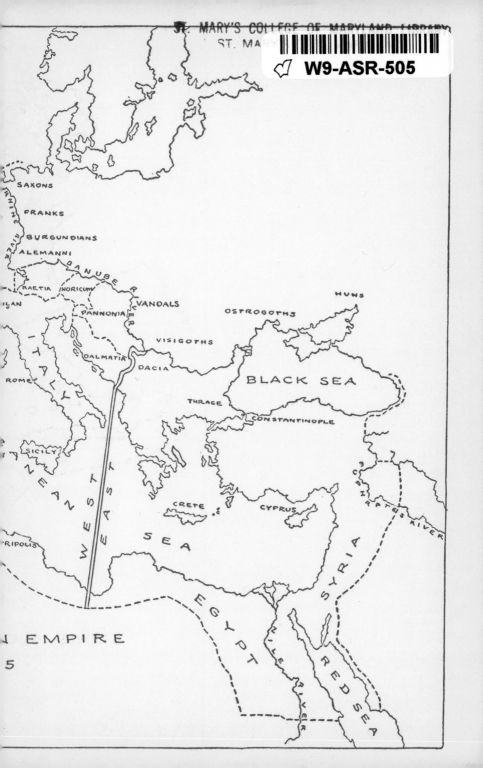

SAXONS

FRANKS

BURGUNDIANS

ALEMANNI

DANUBE R.

RAETIA NORICUM

ILAN

PANNONIA

VANDALS

OSTROGOTHS

HUNS

VISIGOTHS

ITALY

DALMATIA

DACIA

BLACK SEA

ROME

THRACE

CONSTANTINOPLE

SICILY

EUPHRATES RIVER

NEAN

WEST

EAST

CRETE

CYPRUS

SYRIA

RIPOLIS

SEA

N EMPIRE

5

EGYPT

NILE RIVER

RED SEA

Manpower Shortage

and the Fall of the Roman Empire in the West

The Jerome Lectures
Third Series

MANPOWER SHORTAGE

and the Fall of the Roman Empire in the West

by Arthur E. R. Boak

Ann Arbor: The University of Michigan Press — 1955
London: Geoffrey Cumberlege, Oxford University Press

Preface

THE LECTURES on which this book is based were
delivered at the American Academy in Rome in the
autumn of 1951 and at the University of Michigan a
year later; they are now published in accordance with
the provisions of the Thomas Spencer Jerome Foundation. They have been prepared for a wider circle of
readers than the specialists in later Roman history, but
it is hoped that the latter will find the appropriate
sources and modern literature cited in the appended
notes.

For the honor of the appointment to the Jerome
lectureship, I wish to express my sincere thanks to the
committee which administers the Foundation. My
thanks are also due my colleagues and friends at both
the American Academy and the University of Michigan who helped me with friendly criticism and advice
at various stages in the preparation of the lectures
themselves. In this connection, I should like to acknowl-
edge a particular debt to Professor Amos H. Hawley

of the Department of Sociology. I also wish to make grateful acknowledgment of the kindness of Lawrence P. Roberts, Director of the American Academy in Rome, and of Frank E. Brown, Professor-in-charge of the School of Classical Studies, in making available to me the resources and advantages of the Academy during the term of 1951–52, and also of Mrs. Roberts and Mrs. Brown in making the stay at the Academy so very agreeable for Mrs. Boak and myself. And I am very grateful to the editorial staff of the University of Michigan Press, especially to Mr. Walter A. Donnelly, Editor of Official and Museum Publications, for their great care and many helpful suggestions in the preparation of this volume for publication.

A. E. R. B.

Ann Arbor, Michigan
March, 1953

Contents

I

Manpower Shortage in the Late Roman Empire:
An Approach to the Problem

IN BEGINNING this volume on Manpower Shortage and the Fall of Rome, I wish to explain my use
of the terms "Manpower Shortage" and the "Fall
of Rome" as clearly as possible in order to prevent
any misunderstanding of the scope and objective of
my study. First, by the Fall of Rome I mean the
gradual disintegration of the Roman Empire in Italy,
western Europe, and north Africa in the course of the
fifth century of our era. This was the process which
had as its concomitant the rise of Germanic kingdoms
in those areas, and as its inevitable result the transformation of the eastern remnant of the Empire into
a Hellenized, Byzantine state. Second, by Manpower
Shortage I wish to indicate a deficiency in the personnel
necessary to maintain the economic and political struc-
ture of the Western Roman Empire, particularly in
the face of the outside pressures to which it was subjected. Such a shortage might or might not coincide

with, and be the result of, a general decline in population which would be defined as depopulation. Indeed, there might even be an actual increase in total population and yet a shortage of manpower in critical occupation groups. I do not, however, mean to imply that any such increase took place in the Roman state during the period in question.

My interest in the problem of manpower in the Late Roman Empire is of long standing, but it has been aroused to new activity by the recent suggestion of a prominent historian that there was an acute shortage of manpower from the end of the third century, which was caused, not by a decline in population, but rather by the increased demand for suitable personnel.[1] This demand itself was due primarily to the enlargement of the Roman army by the Emperor Diocletian (284–305), which produced a particularly heavy drain on the agricultural population. If I understand this historian correctly, he believes that the population of the Empire was recovering or had recovered from the losses incurred during the disasters of the third century, to which I shall have to refer in more detail on several occasions later in these lectures. He also thinks that the drafting of manpower into the government service under Diocletian and his colleagues and successors produced such a shortage of rural workers that agricultural production fell off to the point where the burden of taxation in kind proved so heavy that there was insufficient food to enable the peasantry to raise families large enough to maintain the population at even a stationary level. Thus, depopulation set in, and this trend became increasingly rapid until the fall of the Western Empire. This is an attractive theory, especially in view of the experience of some modern states in their attempt at reconstruction after World War II. I doubt, however, that it can be substantiated.

In testing this theory I have been led to re-examine the whole question of population trends in the Late Roman Empire, particularly in their relation to manpower shortage. Modern writers are in practically unanimous agreement that there was a steady decline in the population of the Empire during the fourth and fifth centuries and that this had a direct bearing upon the collapse of the western Roman state. The following citations may be taken as representative. J. B. Bury[2] calls the progressive depopulation "the most obvious element of weakness in the Roman Empire." Alfons Dopsch[3] speaks of the "great scarcity of manual labor" in the Empire and holds that this explains the continuous penetration of the Germanic peoples. Even more emphatic is Gustave Bloch,[4] who calls depopulation the most striking feature of the time. And André Piganiol[5] in his recent brilliant work on the period 325 to 395 includes depopulation among the major factors responsible for the Empire's decline. But, so far as I am aware, no one has made a detailed study of the whole problem of the manpower shortage resulting from this depopulation, either as to the time of its inception or in its relation to production, distribution, and the carrying on of essential government services.

As a necessary basis for any study of population problems in the Late Roman Empire, one must form a definite opinion about the state of the population at an earlier date, particularly in the first part of the third century. It is of crucial importance for an interpretation of later population trends to determine whether the population of the Roman world, especially in its western half, was increasing, was in a state of stagnation, or was decreasing before the series of disasters which overtook the Empire in the troublous times between 235 and 284. I am fully aware of the difficulties involved in reaching any definite conclusion on this point, not to speak of one which will command unanimous acceptance, for anyone who deals with the question of population in the ancient Mediterranean world is treading on uncertain ground. He is like a traveler venturing upon a narrow and devious track across a vast swamp beset with treacherous waters and quicksands, guided only by signposts that are few and far between, and even these of doubtful meaning. But this very difficulty presents a challenge. And unless one forms some definite opinions respecting the population of the Roman Empire at several periods in its history, he must be content to develop his interpretation of its social and economic history on an unrealistic basis.

Before proceeding, however, to a discussion of whether the population of the Empire in the period immediately preceding 235 was waxing or waning, I must refer to the supreme difficulty that confronts anyone who attempts to make population studies in the field of ancient history, that is, the almost complete lack of statistics. This lack very sharply differentiates the study of ancient populations from that of populations in modern and, for some areas at least, in medieval times. The distressing absence of exact numerical information was given due emphasis by Julius Beloch in his well-known work *Die Bevölkerung der griechisch-römischen Welt*,[6] which initiated the scientific study of this subject, and no discoveries made since its publication (1889) have materially improved the situation. Not only are statistical figures extremely rare, but most of those which exist admit of more than one interpretation. Who can explain, for example, in thoroughly convincing fashion the extraordinary rise in the Roman census lists between 131 and 125 B.C.? Can anyone say—not with conviction, but with certainty—what persons were included in the number of Romans recorded in the censuses of the time of Augustus? It should be apparent, then, that all general totals given by modern historians or other writers for the population of Italy and the various western provinces or for the Roman Empire as a whole are estimates obtained by using factors such as the size of habitable areas, modern figures of population density, and so on. They may command respect for the ingenuity displayed in their calculation, but not any too great confidence in their accuracy.[7]

The great divergencies in the population figures proposed by different scholars for the Roman Empire in various epochs can thus be understood. Let me cite a few examples. For the time of Augustus at the beginning of the Christian era Beloch[8] allows a total population of from 50,000,000 to 60,000,000; Ferdinand Lot[9] gives 60,000,000 to 65,000,000; and Ernst Stein,[10] about 70,000,000. Here is a difference of some 20,000,000 between the lowest and the highest figures, which is about 40 per cent of the lowest estimate. With regard to the third century an even more striking disagreement is apparent. Delbrück,[11] who is usually very conservative in his numerical calculations (although certainly not here), rates the population about 250 at a minimum of 90,000,000 and considers that it may even have reached 100,000,000. But Stein,[12] who is equally cautious, thinks that it amounted only to some 50,000,000 or about one-fifth of the present population of the same area. J. B. Bury, however, considers the population of the Empire in the time of Constantine I (307–37) to be about 70,000,000.[13] More indefinite is Piganiol,[14] who, although allowing for a rapid decline in the course of the third and fourth centuries, does not believe that as late as 395 the total had dropped to what it was at the beginning of the Augustan era.

Somewhat lesser but still considerable divergencies are noticeable in the computations of the population of the city Rome, regarding which more information is available than for any other city in the Empire. For the time of Augustus, Beloch[15] calculates that the population of the capital was between 760,000 and 810,000; Cardinali,[16] about 930,000; and Kahrstedt,[17] 980,000. For the time of Antoninus Pius (138–61), when the city attained its maximum size, von Gerkan's[18] estimate is between 600,000 and 700,000; Calza and Lugli's,[19] 1,215,000; and Kahrstedt's, 1,250,000, whereas Lot[20] will not admit more than 538,000. As in the case of the conflicting views on the population of the Empire as a whole, the discrepancies here are due to differences in methods of calculation, for example, in the allowances made for such uncertain factors as the slave population, the size of households, the average number of persons residing in each house, and so on.

It is not my purpose to discuss further any of these computations. I have introduced them merely to show that in examining the question of depopulation and manpower shortage in the Roman world one is under the great handicap of having to do without any general population statistics which might serve as a means for measuring the growth or decline of the population as a whole, or even of any classes of it between one period and another. Here, however, it may be worth while to point out that, for reasons which shortly are to be presented, in my opinion the lower estimates of the Empire's total population are to be preferred to the higher.

In particular, one must beware of using modern population figures as a basis for calculating those of the same areas in ancient times. This is because there are, in general, too many variables to be taken into account. For example, there may be a great difference in the type and yield of the cultivated crops, in the farm tools and machinery used, in methods of fertilization and irrigation, in industrial organization, in transportation facilities, in the state of medical science, and in other factors which affect adversely or favorably the number of persons who could or can now live in a given urban or rural area. Only when there is reasonable certainty that conditions of soil, climate, production, distribution, public health, government, taxation, and even religious and moral ideas are approximately

the same can it be admitted that the ancient population may have been about the same as the modern. In
some instances and at certain times it was undoubtedly
greater as, for instance, in lower Mesopotamia, in certain other sectors of the Near East, and in parts of
North Africa. But for the Mediterranean area as a
whole it did not at any time even approximate modern
figures. This is a point of considerable importance
which I shall have to touch upon more fully a little
later.

If I should seem to be too dogmatic in making such
a statement in the light of my insistence upon the lack
of population figures for ancient times, let me say for
the benefit of those who are unfamiliar with the sources
of knowledge of ancient history that for certain regions
there is incontrovertible archaeological evidence for a
rise or decline in population, and for other regions, dependable historical evidence of a nonstatistical nature.[21]

Moreover, in addition to such archaeological and
literary evidence from ancient times, the modern stu-
dent of population problems in the Roman Empire can
avail himself of the results of research in the field of
demographic studies. In recent years, especially, students of population statistics have devoted a great deal
of attention to the ancient world in general and to the
Roman Empire in particular. From ancient writers,
funerary inscriptions, papyri, mummy labels, and even
the skeletal remains in ancient cemeteries they have
garnered quite a surprising amount of information
relative to longevity, birth and death ratios, and the
increase and decline of population. By the critical interpretation of the data obtained in this way, incom-

plete though they are, the demographers have been
able to develop some population patterns, not only for
special areas around the Mediterranean but also for
the Roman Empire as a whole. They have been able,
furthermore, to correlate these patterns with those of
other countries in ancient, medieval, and modern times.
The net result of the establishment of such parallels
between the movements of population in the Roman
world and those of outside countries or parts of the
onetime Roman dominions in later epochs has been to
prove that the Roman experience was not isolated, but
approximated that of other peoples living in a comparable cultural atmosphere. It is justifiable, therefore,
to make use of the known population trends among
such peoples in attempting to trace the demographic
history of the Roman Empire. To the studies in ancient
population statistics some specialists in Roman history
and civilization have made important contributions,
and others have made a more or less limited use of the
work of demographic writers in general. But for the
most part the conclusions of the latter are unknown to,
or have been ignored by, most modern interpreters of
Roman social and economic history. This attitude of
aloofness, however, can no longer be justified, and I
propose to exploit the results of certain demographic
studies as fully as I can in attacking my present problem.

One extremely important result of such studies for
students of Roman population problems is the demon-
stration that only in the course of the last two centuries have European countries experienced any really
great increase in population.[22] This rise has been due in
large part to a phenomenal extension of the average

longevity over that of medieval and early modern times.[23] Other factors are, of course, the technological developments in industry, agriculture, and transportation, which have enabled many more persons to gain a livelihood because of increased production in manufactures and farm products, and also have made it possible to supply the deficiencies of one country from the surpluses of others all over the world. But I shall consider only the great difference in the expectation of life between ancient and modern times. In the more advanced countries of Europe that once were part of the Roman Empire the life expectancy at birth may be placed at over sixty years and in others at about fifty. But for the Roman Empire the corresponding figure was only about twenty-five years.[24] Even for Egypt, which was considered one of the two most populous regions within the Empire, the average age at death was only between thirty-two and thirty-three years, which gives an expectancy at birth of about 23.78 years.[25] In the Roman province of Africa, which was the other area held to have an unusually large population and which enjoyed a relatively favorable death rate, the ancient life expectancy only approximated that of modern India and China,[26] which is less than half that of the more progressive countries of Europe. From figures such as these it is seen that the duration of life in the Roman Empire corresponded to what is known as the Oriental pattern, illustrated by Egypt, India, and China, and not to the Occidental pattern, found in Italy, France, England, and the United States, nor even to that of Greece and Portugal.[27]

The Roman death ratio was somewhat comparable to that which prevailed in England during the period from 1200 to 1450, for which the life expectancy at birth has been calculated with reasonable certainty.[28] For this reason a very brief survey of English population trends in this period seems in place.[29] In 1086 England's population was about 1,100,000. By 1345, before the first onset of the Black Death, it had risen over more than two and one-half centuries to about 3,700,000, but it had fallen to about 2,200,000 in 1377. Not until 1545 had it risen to 3,220,000, still well below the total for 1345. The rise between 1086 and 1345 can be explained in large part by the notable technical advances in agriculture which were made in western Europe in the course of the eighth and following centuries.[30] The decline after 1348 was brought about by the plague commonly known as the Black Death and its consequences, and it is important to note that these consequences did not have their full effects until well after the subsidence of the first great onset of the pestilence and that they continued to be felt for over two hundred years.

Another country in which the life expectancy is roughly the same as in the Roman Empire is China.[31] Like the Roman world, China was, and has remained, a predominantly agricultural area, depending for production upon manpower rather than upon machinery. Like that western world also, China developed a considerable amount of urbanization with a corresponding development of industry and commerce. It might be expected, then, that China's population history would present a pattern very much like that of Rome over a comparable period of time. Enough is known of the population of China from the third century B.C. to the present to warrant the following general outline of its history.[32] This has been "cyclic" rather than "linear." That is to say, it has experienced periods of growth followed by periods of decline. It shows population peaks separated by population lows. Between the beginning of the Roman Empire and our own times, China has experienced five such population cycles with their peaks at approximately A.D. 2; 742–56; 1098–1100; 1573–1620; and 1933. These cycles, it can be seen, were not of equal duration since the peaks were separated by intervals of roughly 750, 350, 500, and 300 years. It may be worth while at this point to consider briefly the stages included within any one of the above-mentioned cycles. They have been described as follows: (1) under the good government of a new dynasty population increases by reason of excess of births over deaths; (2) increased and increasing density of population, coupled with a lack of inventions and technological progress in agriculture, intensifies the struggle for existence; (3) population continues to increase to a saturation point; (4) an era of pestilence and famine accompanied by symptoms of overpopulation begins, ending in war or revolution; (5) population pressure is relieved temporarily, a new dynasty comes into power, but population continues to decrease to a still lower level; (6) population begins to rise again, and a new cycle begins. Is there anything here that can be of help in the interpretation of population trends in the ancient western world? I believe that there is, and I venture to suggest that the cycles of prosperity and decline so evident in the history of Pharaonic Egypt may possibly find their basic explanation in terms of the Chinese experience. But that problem I must leave to the Egyptologists.

For the Roman Empire the parallel is difficult to draw and cannot be pressed very closely. For one thing, the Roman Empire was of much shorter duration than the Chinese and consequently did not experience a similar sequence of population cycles. For another, there was an essential difference in the character of the population in the two areas. Slavery was much more prevalent in the Roman world than in China. There was mass employment of slaves in Roman agriculture and industry, whereas slaves were a negligible factor in these basic occupations among the Chinese. Since the slave population in the Roman Empire did not maintain itself, much less expand, by natural reproduction, an internal population pressure corresponding to those which developed periodically in China was by no means so likely to be built up. One important observation, however, is to be made. Once the Chinese population began to decrease, it continued its downward trend long after the conditions which produced the decline were reversed and conditions favoring a population rise had set in. As has been seen, this delayed recovery is paralleled by the demographic conditions which prevailed in England in the centuries following 1345. In this, at least, I believe that one is justified in drawing upon the Chinese experience to help in determining certain population trends both in the Early and in the Late Roman Empire.

Of particular interest also is another fact established

by statisticians, namely, that in urban centers the birth rate tends to decline until it falls below the death rate. This is true of modern cities both in Europe and in America.[33] The same trend made itself felt even in the smaller towns of medieval times. J. C. Russell[34] remarks: "Population was replaced more rapidly in the villages than in the medieval cities. Since it increased nowhere rapidly, it was not actually replacing itself in the city." There is no good reason for believing that this situation was not characteristic of the cities and towns of the Roman Empire. Obviously, replacement of the urban population comes in modern, as it came in medieval, times through immigration from rural areas. When medieval rural areas could no longer supply the necessary number of immigrants, the urban population decreased. It can hardly be questioned that this was true also of Roman urban centers.[35]

Many persons today seem reluctant to admit the fact that the human population of the world has not increased steadily and continuously since the first appearance of mankind. Indeed, periods of any marked increase have been the exception rather than the rule. It is generally agreed, for example, that in China there has been no material rise in population during the last one hundred years.[36] This should prepare one to accept the possibility of long periods of stagnation in the population of the ancient Mediterranean countries. Roman Egypt, populous though it appeared to be in contrast to other provinces, seems to be a case in point.[37] If so, there must have been many other regions of which the same was true, not to speak of those in which there was a state of decline.

What I have said of some results of demographic studies and their significance for Roman history naturally will seem very elementary to workers in the field of population statistics. But it was necessary for me to call attention to them because, as I have indicated already, I shall try to apply them in my study of manpower shortage in the Late Roman Empire.

Such a study, I feel, must logically begin with a consideration of the state of population in the Empire, especially in its western half, in the early years of the third century. It is a view very generally accepted that the population of the Roman world increased materially under the favorable conditions of the *Pax Romana* established by Augustus and maintained by his successors into the third century of our era. There is, however, some disagreement as to the time when this rise in population came to an end, and a decline, or at least a state of stagnation, set in. Some maintain that the accretion continued until the end of the Severan dynasty in 235,[38] others that a decline began under the Severi between 193 and 235,[39] and still others that this decline had already begun by the time of Marcus Aurelius (161–80).[40] I find myself in agreement with those who support the last of these views. It is unnecessary for me to examine in detail the literary evidence bearing on the state of the population in the Roman world up to the middle of the second century. That has been collected and interpreted by others and is easily available for consultation in their works. Among these I should like to single out as particularly valuable the article of Adolphe Landry, "Quelques aperçus concernant la dépopulation dans l'antiquité greco-romaine," in the *Revue historique* for 1936, because of the use he has made of modern demographic methods in his study. Here I shall limit myself to offering the following considerations in justification of my own conclusions.

In the light of the shortness of life expectancy in the Roman Empire and because of the lack of any evidence of overpopulation, one must conclude that its population pattern conformed to that of medieval and early modern Europe rather than to that of Europe in the last two centuries. Consequently, the population of the Roman world could never have reached very high figures. Certainly, it was never high enough in the opinion of contemporaries. To my mind, one of the strongest proofs of its general deficiency lies in the absence of any population pressures. Admitted that the Roman frontiers were advanced in Britain, central Europe, Syria, and Africa after the time of Augustus, the resultant annexations were made for military or political reasons and never to relieve overpopulation. There was no rush of Romans to take up land in the newly conquered areas. Veterans and their families formed the nuclei of new cities; the rural population was supplied by the natives, who in some cases were forced to abandon a semimigratory pastoral life for a sedentary, agricultural one. Many old cities in Italy and elsewhere increased in size and wealth. But it must be admitted that in Italy, and probably in other parts of the West, a large percentage of the population increase was due to the importation of slave labor for industrial and domestic purposes. In many instances, also, the rise reflected a movement of free persons, particularly merchants and traders, from the eastern provinces or of rural elements attracted from the villages to the towns. Such movements caused a shift in population rather than a total increase. In general, however, this urban growth was not maintained to the end of the second century.

An important factor militating against the rise of population was the extensive use of slave labor both in agriculture and industry. This was particularly true of Italy and Sicily, but other parts of the West were also affected by this practice. Normally, a slave population tends to die out, and Roman slaves were no exception to this rule.[41] During the late Republic and Early Empire the number of slaves in Italy and the western provinces was kept up by the sale of prisoners of war and the importation of slaves from other regions within and without the Empire. The relative infrequency of wars of conquest after the time of Augustus, however, led to a decrease in the supply of captives, and the growing increase in the number of manumissions helped to lower still further the slave population. Some effort was made to breed slaves, but without any great success.[42] The use of slave labor hindered the development of an urban industrial class and also helped the decline of the rural peasantry. In the second century there was a decided shortage of free rural labor. Consequently, the rural areas were in no condition to make good over a long period the natural decrease in the population of the cities.

Another factor which affected the cities in particular was the refusal of the upper and middle classes to raise large families and often even to marry. Against this tendency the laws sponsored by Augustus and maintained in force by his successors with the aim of encouraging families to rear at least three children were pathetically impotent. By the time of Septimius Severus the shortage of population in the middle classes had become a matter of serious concern to the government.[43] Also, unsanitary living conditions, an inadequate diet, and a general lack of medical care combined to keep the death rate high among the poorer urban elements.

Most enlightening on the state of population is the shortage of recruits for the army in the time of Marcus Aurelius. That prudent emperor had to resort to settling conquered Marcomanni within the Empire as landholders under the obligation to supply soldiers to the Roman forces.[44] Apparently, he had no trouble in finding vacant lands on which to place them. And it has been suggested very plausibly that one of the reasons why Aurelius pushed his wars against the barbarians so relentlessly was to effect the recovery of Romans carried off in their raids and so avoid a further increase in untilled lands.[45]

The impoverishment which made itself so widely felt by the time of the Severi also indicates a falling off of population. In the Roman world production depended upon hand labor. Impoverishment meant a decline in production; this in turn implied a shortage of labor, rural or urban or both. It is highly probable that the decline of urban centers in the late second and early third centuries was due, in part at least, to the progressive impoverishment of the surrounding rural areas. And this impoverishment cannot be separated from a decline in the rural population.[46]

Both ancient and modern writers on Roman history have stressed the great loss of life caused by the pest which, beginning in 165 or 166, ravaged the Roman Empire for some fifteen years. But it is too often assumed by modern writers that this loss was rapidly made good and that its effects were not noticeable under the Severi; that, however, is by no means a safe assumption. The experience of England in the fourteenth and fifteenth centuries, referred to above,[47] as well as that of other countries, should indicate that these effects would not be felt in their fullest extent until long after the epidemic itself had subsided. This would mean that the birth rate was being affected adversely at precisely the same time that Septimius Severus and the other rulers of his dynasty were in power.

In view of these conditions, I am persuaded that the decline in population and a related shortage of manpower had already become noticeable at the accession of Septimius Severus in 193. There is evidence of an appreciable decrease under that emperor and his successors until 235.[48] In fact, it may be said that the imperial government accepted shortage of manpower as one of its major problems.[49] By 235, then, the downward trend was definitely established over wide areas, although the rate of decline cannot be computed. It was upon this diminishing population that there fell the catastrophes of the period 235 to 284: continuous rebellion and civil war, devastating barbarian invasions, and a plague which raged even longer than that which occurred during the time of Marcus Aurelius.[50] The impact of these disasters upon a decreasing population must have been tremendous.[51] They not only brought severe losses but also inevitably hastened the rate of decline. There are a few modern scholars who hold that a substantial recovery was made from the losses of these fifty years of disorder in the latter part of the third and the early fourth centuries.[52] If any type of population could have made such a recovery, it would have been a predominantly rural one like that of the Roman world.[53] There is simply no evidence, however, for any substantial rise in population after 284, although one might expect that the rate of decline would diminish, at least temporarily. As has been seen, the experience of England after the plagues of the fourteenth century and that of China after its stages of pestilence and disorder indicate that a downward trend would continue for a considerable period after the re-establishment of conditions favorable to recovery. I believe that this was true of the Late Roman Empire. If such was the case then, there was a resultant shortage of manpower, which would go far to explain the economic and social legislation of Diocletian, Constantine I, and their successors. Whether such a shortage existed and, if so, to what degree it affected production, distribution, and other aspects of life in the western part of the Late Empire is the subject that I propose to examine in detail in the following lectures.

In conclusion, I should like to recapitulate my main points as follows. I hold that it is quite impossible to make any even approximately accurate estimates of the population of the Roman Empire as a whole or of the western part of it in particular, at any specific period. I am convinced, however, that certain definite indications of demographic conditions and trends can be found for different epochs. These conditions, moreover, can be given their safest interpretation in the light of the known population history of other countries and of the laws of population trends worked out by specialists in demography. The application of these analogies and laws in the study of the population of the Early Roman Empire shows that this population was never excessive and that it began to suffer a general decline from the middle of the second century. This decline in turn created a shortage of manpower which was rendered still more acute by the decimation of the population in the course of the troubles of the third century, with the result that the government of the rehabilitated state known as the Late Empire was from the beginning faced with a marked deficiency in its human resources.

II

The Rural Population

IN THE PRECEDING CHAPTER I tried to set forth the population trend in the western part of the Roman Empire from the time of Marcus Aurelius to the accession of Diocletian in 284. As has been seen, the trend had developed a strong downward tendency by 235. That this decline became greatly accelerated during the next fifty years may be regarded as a certainty. Consequently, total population in 284 must have been very much less than at the beginning of this period of chaos. I shall now try to demonstrate how this condition affected the manpower problem of the Late Empire from the point of view of the needs of agriculture, industrial production, and government services. I shall begin with agriculture and the rural population.

At the outset I should like to invite you to consider how the rural classes in particular were affected by the disorders of the third century to which I have re-

ferred.[1] First, there was a series of military revolts
which came with such frequency that they produced a
virtually continuous state of civil war. This can be
appreciated more clearly, perhaps, if one recalls that
between 235 and 284 there were twenty-seven emperors who received official recognition in Rome and
that the number of usurpers who were killed in their
attempts to gain the imperial authority was at least
twice as great. In addition, Gaul, Britain, and Spain
had an independent line of rulers from 260 to 274. A
similar separatist movement developed in the Near
East, although it lasted only about two years (269–
71). It is quite true that with rare exceptions the rebellions were military mutinies, some instigated by ambi-
tious generals, others by the soldiers of different corps
who forced their unwilling commanders to claim the
imperial title. This meant that in most of the actual
fighting only the professional soldiery was involved,
but nonetheless the civilian rural population suffered
very heavily. Apart from those of military age who
were pressed into service, relatively few may have been
killed outright by the rival armies, but a large number
must have perished as an indirect result of the military
operations. There is no evidence that the soldiery
showed any sympathy toward the rural population,
and it is safe to assume that they imitated the conduct
of the Rhineland legions of Vitellius on his march to
Rome in 69.[2] The complete breakdown of discipline
among the Roman troops in the third century would
of itself lead one to think that they would show little
respect for the lives and property of civilians once they
moved out of the areas in which they had long been

garrisoned. This meant that there was constant plundering of the countryside by the armies on the march. Standing crops, if ripe, would be harvested, and stores of food would be taken regularly without compensation; livestock of all sorts would be carried off, and draft animals requisitioned for transport purposes with but little likelihood of their ever being restored to their owners.[3] The net result was impoverishment and starvation in the districts through which the troops moved as well as in those where actual fighting took place.

In the second place, even more disastrous for the rural population in wide areas were the repeated incursions of barbarian raiders who swarmed across the frontiers in great strength when the imperial armies abandoned their role as guardians of the *Pax Romana* in their desire to make and unmake the emperors. In the West the Rhineland, Gaul, Italy, and the upper Danubian provinces bore the brunt of these attacks, but other regions also suffered severely. A few examples will serve to make evident the continuous state of disturbance produced by the barbarian inroads. In 256 the Franks began a series of raids upon the lower Rhineland and Gaul, which lasted over a period of twelve years. During the years 261–64, there were continuous incursions of various Germanic peoples in the same regions. The year 274 again saw Gaul devastated by land and sea, and two years later the whole of that country was again overrun.[4] In Italy the Po Valley suffered a prolonged raid by the Alemanni in 254. Four years later their inroads were carried as far as Rome itself, and in 270 two separate invasions occurred from which a great part of Italy suffered.[5] The province of

Raetia to the north of the Alps was on the line of march for many of the raids into both Gaul and Italy. It was ravaged with particular severity in the years 253, 270–74, and 278.[6] One of the most striking evidences of the serious character of these raids comes in the hasty erection of fortifications for the cities of the threatened or devastated areas, which had been able to dispense with any such protection for two and a half centuries. It is hardly necessary to point out that the construction of Aurelian's great wall for Rome itself in 271 or 272 is the most outstanding evidence of the inability of the imperial armies to ward off the invaders or to contain them in the frontier areas.[7]

The chief brunt of the barbarian incursions was borne by the rural population. It is true that the barbarians sacked scores of towns also, but as a rule they were unskilled in siege warfare, and unless a fortified city was surprised, it had a good chance of warding off an attack.[8] Not so the open villages or isolated farmsteads. And these barbarians were for the most part marauding bands who came to plunder and ravage and not to settle. They showed no hesitation in killing or carrying off into slavery any persons who fell into their hands. In addition to gold and silver, for which they displayed a burning desire, they also made off with other movable spoils such as horses and cattle, not to mention the livestock which they devoured in camp or on the march. If the country people took to the hills or woods or sought refuge behind the nearest city walls on the approach of the barbarians, on their return they found their homes plundered and burned, their farm animals vanished.[9] Thus, for those parts of the Empire which suffered prolonged or repeated devastation of this nature, one must deduce a decline in the numbers of the agricultural population similar to that produced by the operations of the armies of rivals for the imperial authority, but ever so much more serious.[10]

Third, the rural areas were affected by the great plague of the years 250 to 270. Since this epidemic started in the Near East, it most probably struck the eastern provinces more heavily than the western, but the latter did not escape. The movement of troops from the infected areas to other parts of the Empire would of itself help to spread the disease, as it did in the time of Marcus Aurelius. Towns undoubtedly suffered much more heavily than the countryside, but the ravages of the Black Death in Europe among the rural population indicate that the latter had no immunity from such epidemics. Moreover, the preference of the free farm population for a village life under unsanitary conditions to one on isolated farms in Italy and other western lands increased its vulnerability to infection. Thus, losses by disease must be added to those brought upon the agricultural workers by civil war and barbarian inroads.[11]

Finally, among the causes of rural depopulation must be included the flight of tenant farmers and slaves. For the latter, the opportunity to run away in the confusion of a raid was only too tempting, especially if their masters were killed or taken captive. Many slaves were of Germanic stock and welcomed the chance to join roving barbarian bands, but these opportunities occurred only in the areas which were subject to invasion. The flight of the tenant farmers, however, occurred both there and in regions which were spared the horrors of raids. It is quite true, as will be seen, that the emperors of the third century resorted with ever-increasing frequency to the settlement of conquered barbarians as public or private tenants in order to compensate the continuous loss of manpower in agriculture. But it was only to be expected that such colonists would seize the opportunity afforded by the passing of a band of their own or some more or less kindred tribe to regain their liberty. In some cases not even such an inducement was necessary, but merely the weakness of local military and police forces. Witness, for example, the body of Franks settled on vacant lands along the lower Danube under Probus (276–82), who rose in rebellion, seized a number of ships, and after raiding Greece, Sicily, and Africa eventually reached their homeland near the mouth of the Rhine.[12] For the peasantry of the Roman World in general, however, flight was a measure of desperation resorted to only when the burdens imposed on them by the government became intolerable. Conditions were bad enough in some provinces even under the Severi, but in the confusion of the third century they became infinitely worse. The result was that desertions reached alarming proportions. Their extent can be measured by the formation of large bands of brigands, which in some cases constituted veritable armies. Italy became infested with brigands, and under Gallienus (253–68) the movement assumed the aspects of a large-scale rebellion;[13] in Gaul the deserters, known as Bagaudae, terrorized the countryside and menaced the cities, and there were similar troubles in Spain.[14]

As a result of these unfavorable conditions, it must be concluded that the declining agrarian population of the western part of the Empire suffered an additional serious loss of personnel during the critical years 235–84. Weakened in numbers, suffering from poverty and from the resultant malnutrition, its ability to maintain itself by natural reproduction was reduced still further. The manpower shortage in agriculture became more and more acute. Abandoned lands increased to an alarming extent.[15] The only hope of remedying the situation lay in the importation of rural labor from the barbarian world. Accordingly, the emperors felt compelled to resort more and more to this expedient, not always with successful results.[16] Aurelian, for example, planned a large-scale colonization in Italy.[17] It is noteworthy that when he abandoned the province of Dacia to the north of the Danube in 272, he carefully withdrew the Roman civilian population, which he settled in Roman territory to the south of that river.[18] But the third-century emperor most seriously concerned with the problem of reviving agriculture and the rural population was Probus. He settled barbarians in large numbers in Britain, Gaul, Italy, Moesia, and Thrace,[19] a fair indication of the presence of vacant lands and a shortage of farmers and of farm labor throughout all the European provinces of the Empire. Unfortunately, it is only rarely that ancient writers give the numbers of these barbarian colonists. It is said that Probus settled 100,000 Bastarnae in Thrace.[20] Although the accuracy of this figure is questionable because of the general tendency of Roman historians to exaggerate the number of barbarian warriors and captives, at least it indicates a very large number of settlers and a corresponding amount of available unoccupied farm land.[21]

In seeking the objectives of the imperial policy in planting barbarians as agricultural colonists throughout the Empire, it is at times hard to determine whether the dominant motive was to provide for increased agricultural production or to furnish a new source of recruits for the army. One may say, however, that when they were settled on private or imperial estates as slaves or tenants, the desire to ensure increased production and increased revenue predominated; when they were planted in large groups on lands controlled by the emperor, the military interest came to the fore. These were, however, merely two aspects of the same problem, for the rural population was the reservoir of military manpower, and its depletion meant an enfeeblement of the imperial armies. Nothing indicates this more clearly than the abandonment of the triangle between the upper Rhine and the upper Danube, the so-called *Agri Decumates,* and of the province of Dacia. In any case, Probus found the situation so serious that, in addition to settling large numbers of barbarians within the frontiers and actually enrolling barbarians directly in Roman military formations, he employed his soldiers on agricultural projects.[22] All this is proof that the loss in rural manpower had not been made good by the importation of foreign workers when the political and military crisis came to an end and a new era in the history of the Empire began with the accession of Diocletian in 284.

We have next to see whether any improvement in the strength of the agrarian population took place as a result of the stabilization of the government and the reform of the fiscal administration by Diocletian and his colleagues and successors in the last decades of the third and the early part of the fourth century. Here the first question is whether the rural areas enjoyed such a measure of peace and security as to permit a recovery of agriculture and an accompanying improvement in the lot, and consequently in the numbers, of the rural population. There was, indeed, a marked improvement in public security. Rebellions, however, by no means came to an end, although the intervals between them became longer. Between 284 and 395, when the Empire was divided into an eastern and a western half, in the West alone occurred the revolts of Carusius and Allectus (287–93), the wars of the rival emperors (306–24), and the revolts of Magnentius (350–51), Firmus (373–75), Maximus (383–88) and Arbogast and Eugenius (392–94). After 395 the West Roman Empire was torn by the rebellions of Gildo in Africa (397–98), Constantine (406–11), Jovinus (413), Bonifacius (427), and Aetius (432), all of which involved extensive military operations. Nor did the barbarian invasions cease. Various parts of Africa, Britain, Gaul, Raetia, and Upper Pannonia all suffered from raids or more serious invasions during the fourth century. In the fifth century came the invasions and wanderings of the Visigoths, Vandals, Alans, Burgundians, Franks, Alemanni, and Huns, whose combined pressure, added to the forces of internal disintegration, brought about the downfall of the Western Empire.[23] In the face of these disturbances, of both internal and foreign origin, it must be admitted that the rural population in many extensive areas continued to suffer, even if for a time to a lesser degree, from some of the major ills which had hastened its decline between 235 and 284. Although no serious epidemic is noted after the latter date, the effects of that of the middle third century would, if my earlier arguments are sound, still be noticeable in the following centuries. But it might well have been that the surviving agrarian elements, supplemented by renewed barbarian colonization, would ultimately have checked their recession and begun to increase even though at a very moderate rate, if the methods of agricultural operations then in vogue and the imperial fiscal system had been more favorable to the rise of a prosperous and contented class of small landholders, tenant farmers, and rural laborers. Such was far from being the case.

The Late Empire witnessed the culmination of the development of the latifundia, or large estates, which had been going on in the Mediterranean world since Hellenistic times. There was more than a modicum of truth in the statement of Pliny the Elder that the plantations had ruined Italy and were then ruining the provinces.[24] The plantation was a large property operated by the proprietor as a business enterprise, the income from which would enable him to maintain the high standard of living affected by the circle of the nobility and allow him the leisure necessary to engage in public life and to share in the expensive relaxations of the time. Originally, the estate was managed by a steward while the absentee landlord resided in the city of his choice. This remained characteristic of the plantation system in Italy, Sicily, and many other areas. But in Gaul and Britain during the Late Empire the great landlords gave up living in the small impoverished towns and built themselves large country houses on their estates. These properties continued to be operated on the old capitalistic basis, not primarily to supply a comfortable living for the landholder, but to enable him to play a certain political and social role which involved very considerable expenditures. It must never be forgotten, too, that by far the greatest proprietors of all were the emperors, not as private individuals, but as the ones who enjoyed the revenues from the vast complex of estates attached to the imperial office.[25]

Essential to obtaining a satisfactory income from these properties was cheapness of operation. Since methods of agriculture showed little if any improvement between the third century B.C. and the eighth century A.D., production per acre remained constant or fell off wherever the land deteriorated from soil erosion or exhaustion of its mineral content. Cheapness of production, therefore, resolved itself into a question of labor costs. Cheap labor was furnished by slaves as long as they could be obtained at a sufficiently low cost and could readily be replaced when they died or became physically unfit. When in the course of the Early Empire slaves suited to agricultural work became scarcer and more expensive, resort was had more and more to tenant farmers, called *coloni*. These tenants leased small plots of ground from the landlords, which they

cultivated upon payment of a fixed share of their crop
as rental. In addition, they furnished their quotas of
labor for that part of the estate retained by the owner.
At certain seasons of the year, when the labor force
maintained on an estate was insufficient for the work
on hand, casual labor was obtained from nearby towns
and villages. In the fourth and fifth centuries the plantations in the West were operated either by *coloni*
permanently attached to an estate or by slave labor or
by both, with seasonal use, at least in certain areas, of
hired, free labor.[26] At the accession of Diocletian, the
smaller proprietors who lived in the towns and owned
properties in the vicinity had not disappeared, nor had
the small peasant proprietors who lived in village communities. But both of these classes were in process of
being squeezed out by the expansion of the great private estates and the burdens imposed upon them by the
imperial government in the form of taxes, requisitions,
and forced services.

The land tax reform begun by Diocletian in 287 but
not completed until 312 also had a very direct bearing
upon the welfare of the rural population of the Late
Empire.[27] Under the new system both the land and the
persons who worked it were subjected to taxation. In
each province the land was divided into units of sup-
posedly equal productive capacity. Each of these units
seems to have been equated for purposes of taxation
with one agricultural worker. Hence, at first both the
land and the human units, paying equal taxes, were
known as *capita*. Later on, the land unit came in general to be known as a *iugum*. Primarily because of the
instability of the coinage, Diocletian, in his desire to

secure a constant and adequate flow of provisions for his troops, levied his new land taxes entirely in kind and not in money. His intention, no doubt, was to protect the farmers from such requisitions as had been made irregularly and arbitrarily by his predecessors in the third century to compensate for the deficiencies in the regular revenues. But the amount of the new tax on each unit did not vary with fluctuations in the yield of the annual crops; the government collected it at a rate fixed in advance in accordance with its estimated needs for a period known as an indiction. The Christian author Lactantius, writing about 307, claims that as a result of the immense load of the indictions the resources of the tenant farmers were exhausted and they deserted their fields.[28] On the other hand, Aurelius Victor, who is more impartial, asserts that at first the land tax was bearable but that in the course of time it proved ruinous.[29] Since Victor wrote in 360, and there is no evidence for any great increase in the total budget of the Empire between the time of Diocletian and that date, the mounting burden of the land tax must have been due to other factors, in particular, a decrease in production and oppressive methods of tax collection. A falling off in production meant a continuous decrease in the amount of cultivated land, which in turn implied a decrease in the number of persons engaged in agriculture. That more and more land did go out of cultivation is attested by the government's resort to the practice of *epibole* or *adjectio*.[30] Under this system abandoned lands that formerly had been taxed were assigned to the proprietors or tenant farmers of adjacent towns and villages or to neighboring large estates for cultivation and payment of the land tax. That this proved in many cases an intolerable burden is seen in the repeated laws issued on the subject by emperors of the fourth and fifth centuries. And the main reasons for its being so were shortages of available farm labor and of capital. The result was that many cultivators abandoned their properties rather than face the danger of receiving forced allocations of vacant land.

That Diocletian's method of taxing farm lands contained in itself the seeds of future inequities is beyond question.[31] It was rendered much worse by the injustice, greed, and corruption of the tax assessors and tax collectors, for which there is abundant contemporary evidence. Those who suffered most from these abuses were the free small landholders and tenant farmers, whose condition was rendered so intolerable that they found their properties confiscated for arrears of taxes or took to flight in fear that they would be sold out.[32] Under such conditions of land tenure and rural taxation no opportunity to recover from a progressive decline was given to that part of the agrarian population which had managed to survive the crisis of the third century.

There is still another factor which contributed to the depopulation of rural areas in the western provinces of the Empire. This was malaria. It was inevitable that this disease, endemic in parts of Italy since the sixth century B.C., should spread *pari passu* with the increase in abandoned lands, which resulted in the neglect of drainage installations and the consequent formation of more extensive marshy areas that afforded optimum conditions for the breeding of malaria-carrying mosquitoes. At a certain point malaria was bound to work as a cause as well as an effect of depopulation, both by increasing the number of deaths and by sapping the vitality of the survivors in the infected areas. I do not wish to overemphasize the role of malaria in this respect. Not all of the western provinces were affected by this scourge. On the basis of the later history of malaria in European lands, it may be assumed that the more northerly areas suffered very little from it. On the other hand, central and southern Italy, as well as Sardinia and parts of Sicily and Spain, probably incurred noticeable losses.[33]

At this point it will be useful to undertake a brief survey of agrarian conditions in the western parts of the Empire from the time of Diocletian to the collapse of the imperial authority in the West as they are revealed in the literary and archaeological evidence. For Britain [34] what information exists is drawn almost entirely from archaeological discoveries. These show first of all that at no time in either the Early or Late Empire was the population of the part of the island occupied by the Romans very numerous. The area brought under cultivation was restricted largely to the lighter soils, which were easily cleared of their thinly growing woodlands. Little progress was made in cutting back the thick forests of the heavier and more productive clay soils. This points to a stationary agricultural population, under no pressure to extend the limits of the productive area, especially if, as some maintain, the heavy gang plough capable of turning clay soils was known to the Romanized Britons. During the late third and early fourth centuries the towns in Britain fell into decay and failed to regain their earlier population and prosperity. In the same period the number of villas or homes of the larger land-holders which showed signs of considerable prosperity greatly increased. This points to a migration of the provincial nobility from the depopulated towns to their country estates. In other words, the agricultural sys-tem in Britain in the Late Empire rested mainly on large estates tilled by *coloni,* slaves, or other depend-ents. As I have pointed out, this plantation system was the reverse of favorable to the expansion of the agrarian population, particularly under an oppressive fiscal regime such as that of the Late Roman Empire. That British agriculture in this period was not very productive is revealed by a lack of any large-scale ex-port of wheat, its major crop. It is true that the Em-peror Julian in 357 temporarily provisioned the towns which he restored in the Rhineland with British wheat, but since this was procured by a forced levy and not by purchase in an open market, it cannot be taken to indicate a regular surplus of grain.[35] On the other hand, Britain did export woolen garments, which it had not done earlier. This points to an extension of sheep raising, which required far fewer farm hands than were needed for tillage. Elsewhere in the ancient world expansion of the sheep industry indicated a decline in the area of cultivated land and an accompanying de-crease in the rural population, interacting as cause and effect. It may well be suspected that such was also the case in Britain.[36] But much of this is speculation. In-dicative of late third-century conditions is the fact that

Probus found room to settle a considerable number of Frankish prisoners of war as farmers on the island. The archaeological record shows that in the second half of the fourth century the country villas experienced a marked decline in prosperity and in numbers. Evidence is lacking as to whether barbarian raids or internal conditions contributed most to this deterioration. At least there are definite indications of decline in the strength of the rural population.

For the Gallic provinces [37] there is perhaps more information regarding rural conditions than for any other part of the Western Empire. This is due to the survival of a considerable quantity of contemporary literature which supplements and helps to interpret the abundant archaeological evidence. Of particular importance are the works of writers who lived or at least wrote in Gaul. Among these are the authors of the panegyrics addressed to Maximian (289), Constantius (297), Constantine I (310 and 311), Constantine Caesar (321), Julian (362), and Theodosius I (389), besides such well-known writers as the fourth-century rhetorician Ausonius of Bordeaux and the fifth-century writers Sidonius Apollinaris, bishop of Auvergne, and Salvian, a presbyter of Marseilles. Among non-Gallic authors are the eminent historian Ammianus Marcellinus, who campaigned in Gaul during the years 354 to 357, and others of lesser importance.

In Gaul the disorders of the period 235 to 284 had left in their wake a trail of ruined cities and an empty and desolated countryside. The agricultural population had almost disappeared; part had been killed, part carried into captivity, and part had deserted their fields to form large and well-organized bands of brigands locally known as Bagaudae.[38] The question to be answered is: Did rural Gaul experience a recovery from this devastation, and was its farming population restored to such an extent that it was able to meet the public and private demands upon agriculture?

If one were to rely solely upon Ausonius and Sidonius, he would have to answer this question in the affirmative. For both describe a rich and cultivated society supported by vast estates which produced grain and wine in great abundance. There is no hint of any shortage of agricultural labor and hardly a reference to agrarian troubles of any sort. In fact, the tillers of the soil are ignored to an even greater extent than are the barbarians who were slowly but surely undermining the Empire in the West. No hint of the coming collapse of the Empire appears in the works of either of these writers.[39] But it must be remembered that they belonged to the upper social and economic class and addressed their works to others who moved in the same circles. Perhaps one might see some confirmation of the view that the recovery in agriculture was quite satisfactory in a statement in the curious little work known by the exaggerated title *Description of the Whole World* (*Expositio totius mundi*) to the effect that Gaul has everything in abundance, but at very high prices. It must, however, be remembered that this is a fifth-century Latin version of a Greek work of the middle fourth century whose author had no personal acquaintance with the western part of the Empire.[40] Moreover, "has everything in abundance" is one of his stock generalizations applied at times to regions known to be in a state of economic decline.

A very different account is presented by other sources which reveal the conditions that prevailed among the middle and lower classes engaged in agricultural pursuits. After the suppression of the Bagaudae by the Emperor Maximian in 286 and the consequent restoration of internal security, there was unquestionably a revival of agriculture. In large part this was brought about by the settlement of captive barbarians as obligatory tenants on the properties of the landholders.[41] This revival, however, does not seem to have been either universal or continuous. When Constantine I visited the city of Autun (*civitas Flavia Aeduorum*), the territory of which comprised a rich agricultural area, he found its land tax five years in arrears. This was said to be due to the fact that the farmers found the rate of taxation so heavy that they could no longer stand the expenses involved in tilling their fields and so had deserted them. Consequently, the emperor canceled the delinquent taxes and reduced the number of tax units (*capita*) from 32,000 to 25,000.[42] This was a reduction of more than one-fifth of the previous assessment, and one is tempted to think that it corresponded to a decrease in the number of tillers of the soil. At the same date, however, the territories of other cities appear to have been in a more flourishing condition.[43]

About the middle of the fourth century the general situation in Gaul had once more deteriorated. Brigandage had again assumed dangerous proportions and was destined to remain a scourge until the end of Roman

rule.[44] As in the third century, the chief source of recruits for these bands of Bagaudae continued to be
agricultural workers who deserted their fields because
of the oppression of landlords or tax collectors. The
barbarians had renewed their raids. In 355 forty or
fifty cities were pillaged by the Alemanni, Franks, and
Saxons.[45] It is true that order was restored temporarily
by the Caesar Julian in the years 357–60, and later by
the emperors Valentinian I and Theodosius I, but further raids continued for the rest of the fourth century.[46] In the early fifth century began the great invasions of whole peoples which led to the permanent
occupation of Gaul by the Franks, Visigoths, and Burgundians and its gradual loss to the Empire.[47] In addition, Gaul was the scene of revolutions and civil wars
which increased the general insecurity and resulted in
loss of life and property.[48] Contemporary writers re-
marked, and imperial legislation confirmed their observation, that the farm workers, particularly those of
barbarian origin, were only too eager to seize the opportunity afforded by the passing of a band of invaders
to abscond and join the raiders.[49] The latter also continued the practices of their predecessors of the third
century and carried off large numbers of captives and
great quantities of movable goods.[50] In such a situation there could be no permanent improvement in agricultural conditions. Julian's inability to find enough
wheat in Gaul to supply the temporary needs of the
garrison cities which he restored along the Rhine in 357
and the references of Ausonius to the possibilities of
famine [51] indicate definitely that the production of
grain, at least, remained at a low level.

Some modern historians have argued that the settlement of barbarians as slaves, *coloni,* or military colonists within the Empire, and particularly in Gaul, reversed the downward trend in the rural population and by virtue of their higher birth rate brought about a rise in population.[52] But this is belied by the continued increase in abandoned lands, the progressive decline in the population of western Europe between 200 and 900,[53] the constant demand on barbarian manpower for agriculture in Gaul, and the ability of the invading barbarian tribes to find room for themselves without any serious displacement of the existing population.[54] It may be concluded, therefore, that Roman Gaul continued to suffer from a deficiency of agricultural labor up to the time when it passed under barbarian control.

Regarding agricultural conditions in the provinces of the upper Rhine and upper Danube—Raetia, Vindelicia, and Noricum—there is practically no information for the period of the Late Empire. But the frequency of barbarian incursions into and through these areas as well as the progressive abandonment of the Roman frontier defenses to the north of the Alps justifies the conclusion that the rural population was sparse and had experienced no recovery from the losses of the third century.[55] There is a similar dearth of evidence for the islands of Corsica and Sardinia. The former of these never attained any notable amount of agricultural productivity, but Sardinia has considerable arable land and in earlier times had been able to export grain in quantity, although largely in payment of taxes levied by the Roman government.[56] The spread of the latifundia system on the island, however, and the ultimate absorption of the great private estates by the imperial domains presumably resulted here as elsewhere in a decrease of the rural population.[57] In any event, the population of the island was never large in ancient times,[58] and the difficulty of maintaining cultivation on the imperial lands in the time of Constantine I points to a decrease in the course of the third and early fourth centuries.[59] Nor is there any evidence for an improvement in demographic conditions during the whole period of the Late Empire.[60] The prevalence of tax delinquency in the time of Constantius and Constantine [61] indicates worsening conditions in agriculture, and when in 363 Julian abolished the requisitioning of post horses for the public post in Sardinia as being too burdensome for the "rural plebs" [62] one may suspect this was due as much to the poverty of this class as to the abuses of the post system itself. Sardinia continued to export wheat but, more significantly, also sent pork and mutton to the Roman market, although these products probably represented taxes in kind and requisitions rather than a true surplus of production at the disposal of the landholders.[63] On the basis of these scanty references, it must be concluded that the rural population of Sardinia remained weak until the Vandal conquest in 455.

Although the remaining island province, Sicily, was much richer agriculturally than Sardinia and economically was of greater importance to the city Rome, very little is known about conditions there from the third to the fifth centuries.[64] It had become a land of great estates, imperial and private, tilled largely by slave labor, and there had been a corresponding decline in the free agrarian population.[65] Agriculture remained the basis of its economic life; it was one of the granaries of the Roman Empire in the West; its wool and its horses were also important as exports.[66] In spite of this, Sicily experienced a general economic decay under the Late Empire, accompanied by a decrease in total population,[67] which necessarily involved the manpower available for agricultural operations.

The condition of the agrarian population in the provinces of the Spanish peninsula during the Late Empire is even more obscure than that in Sardinia and Sicily. The *Expositio* speaks of various agricultural products, notably olive oil, pork, esparto grass for ropes, and horses.[68] This implies considerable activity in agriculture, but as with other provinces, it must be assumed that much of the export trade really consisted in the movement of government goods raised by taxation or forced sale. It cannot be conceded, however, that Spanish agriculture in this period was as flourishing as during the first and second centuries of the Empire, for in the fourth century the south coast was only sparsely inhabited.[69] There must, therefore, have been a decrease in the farming population, which may be connected with the decline of the Spanish municipalities after the second century. It is legitimate to doubt that there was any substantial recovery before the barbarian settlements in the fifth century.

In North Africa the provinces belonging to the western part of the Empire enjoyed prosperous conditions with a rural population that increased or certainly held its own until the disorders of the third century.[70] In spite of devastation due to civil war and the rebellions and invasions of native tribes in the period 235 to 284, prosperity continued in various areas into the fourth century.[71] In agriculture the great estates, both private and imperial, dominated the scene.[72] The chief agricultural exports were grain and oil; camels, horses, and sheep were raised in great numbers.[73] Here, again, it is safe to conclude that the exported grain and oil were in large part collected as taxes and transported for public uses. Yet the general situation in Roman Africa throughout the fourth and the first half of the fifth centuries was unfavorable to the maintenance of a flourishing rural economy and a strong agrarian population. The raids of the Berber tribes continued and at times assumed dangerous proportions; official corruption and oppression were rampant; two serious rebellions affected wide areas.[74] And this was not all. The rural areas were kept in a state of continual disturbance by the activities of the Circumcelliones, bands of itinerant farm laborers who, like the Bagaudae in Gaul, sought relief from their miseries in acts of violence against the properties and persons of the well-to-do. Their allegiance to the heretical sect of the Donatists gave their movement the character of a national religious as well as social revolt,[75] and the attempts of the government to suppress the Donatist clergy increased still further the internal confusion. Under these conditions one should expect to find a decrease in the manpower available for agricultural purposes. The proof that a severe shortage developed is to be found in the alarming increase of abandoned farms on the imperial domains. In 422, of the domains in the province of Africa Proconsularis, about one-third had ceased to be cultivated, and of those in the adjacent province of Byzacena more than one-half were untilled.[76]

Having surveyed the state of the agrarian population in the western provinces, I shall now turn to Italy. Here, too, the evidence is not too abundant but is, nonetheless, quite convincing. Italy was pre-eminently a land of great estates, given over largely to grazing and the cultivation of vineyards. Since the time of Marcus Aurelius, its supply of rural labor had at best been inadequate and became much more so as a result of the plague and military disturbances of the third century. There is no sign of an improvement in the Late Empire. In fact, everything points to a progressive deterioration. Brigandage, that symptom of an impoverished and fugitive rural population, was rife even in the vicinity of Rome itself.[77] Malaria became a scourge in Tuscany,[78] as it had been for a long time in Latium and elsewhere. The valleys of the northern Apennines gave an impression of desolation to Bishop Ambrose in 387, and Symmachus complained of the mournful appearance of the Italian countryside.[79] It is true that the *Expositio* speaks of Calabria as producing wheat, Bruttium much excellent wine, Lucania quantities of pork, and of Campania as the storehouse of Rome.[80] Imperial legislation of the fourth and fifth centuries indicates that Lucania, Samnium, and Campania all were important swine-raising areas.[81] But all this is indicative of an absence of intensive farming, and, in fact, Italy did not produce enough to supply its own needs, for in spite of the steady diminution of the population of Rome that city was forced to depend upon importations of food stuffs from Africa, Sicily, and Sardinia. Unlike most of the western provinces, the Italian peninsula did not suffer from invasions during the fourth century, but in the years 408 to 412 it was ravaged by the Visigoths under Alaric and Ataulf, whose depredations fell most heavily on the rural areas.[82] Following the example of the slaves of Rome, the barbarians on the private estates doubtless embraced this opportunity to desert and gain their freedom. Even before this disastrous episode the Emperor Honorius in 395 removed from the tax rolls of Campania 528,052 *iugera* (about 352,000 acres) of land once cultivated but now untilled and abandoned.[83] If this was the situation in Campania, the richest agricultural region in the peninsula, conditions in other districts must have been even worse. Here is irrefutable testimony to the attenuation of the rural population in Italy. Confirmatory evidence comes in the settlement of a large number of Alemanni on fertile lands in the Po Valley in 370,[84] and in the opposition of a typical large landholder like Symmachus to furnishing recruits for the army from his tenants.[85]

From the foregoing survey of the western provinces and Italy, one gains a comprehensive view of a continuous decline in agricultural production and of an agricultural population that grew steadily weaker in numbers. This general condition explains the concern of the imperial government over the shortage of farm labor and the falling off of revenues derived from the land taxes as evidenced by the legislation contained in the *Theodosian Code;* compiled in 438, and its supplements, the *Novellae* of Theodosius II, Valentinian III,

Majorian, Severus, and Anthemius, dated between 438 and 468. This legislation must now be examined in order to see what light it throws upon the problem of shortage of manpower in agriculture.

Of primary importance in this respect is the fact that by the early fourth century the small tenant farmers, known in general as *coloni,* who formerly had enjoyed freedom of movement and freedom of contractual relations with their landlords, were legally bound to the farms which they cultivated and passed with them from one owner to another. In other words, they had become serfs. And this condition applied equally to those on the public or imperial domains and those on private estates. It is unnecessary here to go into the much discussed question of the origin of this type of serfdom, commonly known as the colonate.[86] Suffice it to say that for most of the Empire, including all of the western part, the system was firmly established by the time of Constantine I.[87] But it must be of earlier date and should in all probability be ascribed to Diocletian, for it was the logical consequence of his reform of the land tax that, if the taxes were to be paid in agricultural products, the lands must have labor to work them.[88] If the shortage of agricultural labor was acute and becoming increasingly serious, the government must intervene and see that the fields of the landlord were tilled. Such a shortage was the inevitable result of the decline of the rural population, particularly during the period 235–84. The government's resort to fixing the peasants to the soil which they tilled is proof both that the shortage existed and that there was no prospect of a rise in the rural population which would make good the defect within any reasonable time. Not only did the state have to attach the *coloni* to the land, but it also had to be sure that they remained there and did not seek to engage in different occupations or transfer themselves to properties other than those to which they had been assigned. Accordingly, in 332 Constantine I ordered that any proprietor who knowingly held a *colonus* from the estate of another on his own property should restore him to his original estate and that the *colonus* himself should be reduced to slavery.[89]

It was not enough to bind an individual *colonus* to a farm; some provision had to be made for his ultimate replacement; therefore, the wife and family of each such peasant were bound with him to the land which he tilled. Thus, the colonate became a hereditary status. The lot of these obligatory tenants proved so unsatisfactory that they continually sought to escape from it. They tried to enter the army, the Church, the civil service, or other professions. Some even attempted to transfer themselves to the estates of other proprietors in the hope of improving their condition. Since, however, the shortage of rural labor continued and even became accentuated, the emperors could not relax their restrictions, and they issued repeated laws recalling the refugees to their original habitat and obligations.[90] Only if a male *colonus* who had absconded escaped detection for a period of thirty years, could he expect to be liberated from his hereditary bonds. If detected within that interval, he and his children and all his personal belongings were restored to his former master's estate. If he had died, his children, with their own property and their father's as well, went back to the original

proprietor. For a woman, the corresponding period
was twenty years. If, however, she had married and
was living with a *colonus* bound to another proprietor-
ship, and if she were discovered within the twenty-year
period, she could be recovered together with one-third
of her offspring by her original patron, although her
new patron was permitted to send a substitute for her
and to compensate the former patron for her children.
If she had married a free man of any other status, she
and all of her children must be returned to her place
of origin.[91]

Not only did the former small tenant sink to the
status of a serf, but the same fate overtook the free
agricultural worker, the *inquilinus,* in the course of the
fourth century. He, too, lost his freedom of movement
and became permanently attached to the estate on
which he was employed. By the fifth century there was
no practical distinction between him and the *colonus.*[92]
Bound to the soil also were the barbarian captives who,
under the name of *tributarii,* were assigned as agricultural laborers to individual proprietors, not as slaves
but as serfs subject to a head tax.[93] Even though the
number of slaves steadily decreased during the Late
Empire, they continued to form an important element
among the agricultural workers.[94] The government, in
its anxiety to maintain a supply of farm labor, restricted the freedom of the owner to dispose of the
slaves who worked his fields, usually like the *coloni,*
as occupants of separate farms. They could not be sold
apart from the estate where they had been employed.[95]
Every effort was made to prevent slaves from abscond-
ing or being enticed away and concealed by persons in

need of labor, conditions which were chronic and called forth repeated prohibitions from the emperors.[96] In this connection, a law of 382 provided that able-bodied beggars, if runaway slaves, could be held in slavery by the one who denounced them, but if of free birth, they should become perpetual *coloni* of their discoverer.[97]

So much for the tenants who tilled their leaseholds and the laborers who cultivated the fields of others. Was there an equivalent decrease in the number of petty proprietors who worked their own lands and formed villages of free peasants in various parts of the empire?[98] It must be concluded that their numbers declined as did those of the *coloni,* for they continued to suffer from the encroachments and competition of the larger proprietors as they had in the Early Empire, and they were much less able to defend themselves against the oppression of the tax collectors and other government officials.[99] As for the middle-class landowners, who for the most part were residents of towns and cities and cultivated their lands through *coloni* or other hereditary tenants or slaves, they do not fall into the class of rural workers. Their situation will be discussed in the following chapter.

The failure of the agrarian policy of the Late Empire is vividly portrayed by the steady increase in the extent of abandoned agricultural land, the continuous resort to the *epibole,* and the constant necessity of remitting arrears of land taxes. The extent of deserted lands in Africa and Campania which had to be dropped from the tax rolls has already been noted. Also, the legislation of the fourth and fifth centuries shows that the problem of the *agri deserti* was both serious and continuous throughout the whole Empire.[100] In 365 vacant lands were distributed to veterans and to foreign tribes, and occupants of such lands were to enjoy a three-year exemption from taxes and rents.[101] The emperors Valentinian and Valens gave permission to all who so desired to occupy lands of the Private Purse (Crown Lands) in all the provinces subject only to regular taxation.[102] In 386 another constitution declared that all persons who cultivated and stocked abandoned lands belonging to the Patrimonial Domain (the inherited property of the emperors) should hold them in private ownership subject to the land tax. But waste land and poorer land had to be taken up along with good lands or added to such as had been made productive, and even those who held poorer lands were made responsible for taxes on waste lands. Those who did take up abandoned lands, however, were given an exemption from taxes for three years.[103] Again, in 391, the Emperor Theodosius I promised that anyone who cultivated abandoned lands should obtain full title to them after two years.[104] A constitution issued by Valentinian and Valens declared that throughout Italy every taxpayer was bearing the burden of an additional payment for land abandoned by others.[105] Delinquent land taxes were remitted occasionally in the early and middle fourth century, but from 395 this was done with such frequency as to justify the view that there was a general breakdown of the agricultural system in the western half of the Roman world.[106]

In the light of the foregoing evidence for the scarcity of manpower in agriculture and the increase in abandoned lands, one may well ask why the administration had to protect itself against usurpations of imperial farms and estates, and why any persons at all wanted to acquire more land, as was actually the case.[107] The answer is that the greater landholders, members of the official aristocracy or closely related to it, were able to operate their large properties more successfully than the smaller proprietors because they did not need to cultivate their land intensively and could get along with a relatively small number of workers. All the more so if, as so often happened, they were able to acquire properties without payment. Furthermore, owing to their influence and to collusion with local tax authorities, they contrived to avoid paying much of their quota of the land taxes. Consequently, they were anxious to expand their domains at the expense of the imperial and municipal properties or those of the lesser landowners. Even tenants on the imperial domains were willing at times to take over deserted land, if it was of good quality and they could acquire it on favorable terms of tenure and taxation. After all, land was the only form of wealth that they could accumulate, and farming the only method of gaining a livelihood that they knew.

It is important to note that even the senatorial order, made up of the wealthiest landowners of the Empire, had trouble in keeping their lands under cultivation. In 384 the senators from Macedonia, like those from Thrace, were exempted from paying the special senatorial land tax, the *collatio glebalis,* which was a money tax imposed in addition to the ordinary land tax in kind;[108] in 393 other senators were complaining that they could not meet this levy[109] and at the same time inferior provincial lands were being abandoned by the aristocracy.[110] It was admitted by the emperors in 397 that in some provinces half of the senatorial taxes were in arrears,[111] but this seems to have been due rather to their ability to resist the tax collectors than to their inability to pay the *collatio*. In 417 senators who took over abandoned properties were exempted from paying the senatorial tax thereon, even if the estates concerned had formerly been subject to it.[112] Since the *collatio glebalis* was a sort of super-tax which was levied upon the higher-ranking and presumably richer senators at a higher rate than on those of lower rank and lesser properties, it is tempting to see in the complaints against it a failure in production rather than a lack of capital. Low production in agriculture was, in turn, the result of primitive methods and lack of manpower. Even if this inference is not fully justified, I think that it is safe to believe that the greater proprietors were the ones who were guilty of enticing away or harboring *coloni* and slaves belonging to other properties.

All classes of landholders, then, suffered, although to varying extent, from a creeping paralysis in agriculture attributable in large part to that *raritas colonorum*,[113] "the scarcity of farm workers," which afflicted the western part of the Roman world throughout the whole period of the Late Empire.

III

The Urban Population

IN THE second chapter I discussed the shortage of manpower in the rural population of the western half of the Late Roman Empire. I shall now try to trace the demographic history of the contemporary inhabitants of the towns, whose fortunes were so closely interwoven with those of their rural neighbors, in order to see if any evidences of a deficiency in the number of persons available for industrial, commercial, and other urban activities are to be found. First, I shall summarize what is known about the general condition of the towns of this period and then discuss certain classes of the population of Rome and of the provincial cities about which some specific information is available.

The population of the towns, like that of the rural districts, was already declining when it was exposed to the sufferings of the period 235–84.[1] Since I have dwelt upon these troubles in considerable detail,[2] it will not be necessary to describe them any further; I shall merely point out in what ways the urban population was affected by them. Naturally, it suffered very heavy losses from the great plague which began about 250.[3] As among the rural residents, the effects of this epidemic were bound to be felt in the cities long after its subsidence.[4] Certainly, too, a number of municipalities suffered destruction or pillage in the struggles between rival contenders for the imperial power.[5] All without exception, it may be affirmed, were laid under heavy contributions for the maintenance and the movements of the imperial armies as well as those of the would-be usurpers. This meant a severe drain upon the resources of the urban population, which in many areas were showing signs of depletion even before 235.[6] Nor did the barbarian raids fail to take a heavy toll of the inhabitants of the towns and of their wealth. It is quite true that on many occasions the walled towns were able to ward off direct assaults,[7] but the outlying properties belonging to the residents of even these communities suffered from ravaging and burning by the plundering bands. Moreover, in the Rhineland, along the upper Danube, and in the greater part of Gaul, areas which bore the brunt of the Germanic incursions, there can hardly have been a single town which did not fall at least once into the hands of the barbarians. For example, in the year 275 alone sixty towns of Gaul were said to have been captured and plundered by various barbarian tribes.[8] From these towns much wealth in gold, silver, and other portable objects was carried off, other property suffered serious damage, and great numbers of the people themselves were dragged away into captivity.[9] One can hardly exaggerate the effects

of the general state of disorder upon the economic condition of those people in the cities who lived by commerce and industry. The roads were unsafe because of
brigands, barbarians, and troops on the march. The
seas became infested with pirates. Under these circumstances manufactured goods could not be exported beyond the locality in which they were made, and merchants had great trouble in importing wares from distant regions. Consequently, the classes which previously
had prospered by industrial and commercial activities
were ruined, and this increased still further the impoverishment of their native cities.[10]

The effects of this prolonged crisis are seen in a general decline in the size and prosperity of the cities of
the Late Empire when compared with their condition
in the period preceding 235. Archaeologically, this
shrinkage and impoverishment is widely attested, although for lack of systematic excavations the evidence
is by no means complete for all the western parts of the
Empire. In Britain, from the latter part of the third
century the area occupied by the towns whose sites have
been studied was considerably less than it had been
under the Early Empire. Also, the buildings were
smaller and correspondingly cheaper in construction.
Here there are strong indications of a decline both in
population and in wealth.[11] From Gaul the evidence is
very much clearer and more abundant. There, as has
been seen, most of the urban communities had been
sacked in the course of the third century by barbarians,
brigands, or rebellious Roman troops. When the towns
were rebuilt, they were fortified or refortified by walls
which date from the end of the third or from the early

fourth century. But these walls, whose circuits in many cases may still be traced, with rare exceptions enclosed only a fraction, and in some instances a very small one, of the former urban area.[12] As has been observed, many of the rebuilt cities had contracted to the bounds of the earlier Celtic villages from which they had grown in the first, second, and early third centuries. There can be no doubt that this shrinkage in size represents a corresponding shrinkage in population. According to A. Grenier: "From the time of Postumus apparently the town had become a *castrum* or fortress able to shelter a garrison, government officials, some clergy and a small population of merchants." [13]

But how can this account, based on archaeological evidence, be reconciled with the descriptions of the flourishing condition of certain Gallic towns given by Ammianus Marcellinus, by the author of the *Expositio Totius Mundi*, and by Ausonius in his *Order of Famous Cities (Ordo Urbium Nobilium)*? For one thing, these descriptions are comparative, not with past conditions but with those of the writers' own time. Certain cities are selected for praise because they stand out among their contemporaries, not because of the contrast with their own condition in an earlier, more flourishing period. Moreover, these descriptions are very general and give no statistical information regarding size, wealth, or other matters of importance. As for Ammianus, a soldier, the state of a city's defense apparently was an important factor in winning his favorable comment.[14] The *Expositio* singles out only two Gallic cities for special mention, Augusta Treverorum (Treves) and Arles.[15] Ausonius includes five in his list of twenty famous cities from the whole Empire, but his choice seems heavily weighted in favor of his native Gaul. The five towns selected by him are Treves, Arles, Toulouse, Narbonne, and his own birthplace, Bordeaux.[16] With respect to Treves, it is highly probable that it had actually experienced an increase in population during the early fourth century. It had become an imperial residence, the seat of administration for Gaul, Britain, and Spain. Consequently, it came to be adorned with an imperial palace, large public baths, and other buildings worthy of its political importance. Treves was also a strongly garrisoned city; here were civil administrative bureaus with a numerous personnel. Here, too, were located important government arsenals and factories and an imperial mint. The importation of supplies of various kinds for the soldiers and civil servants, as well as articles of luxury for the court and high officials, required the presence of a numerous urban element engaged in transportation and distribution.[17] In the Late Empire, Arles was the chief Mediterranean outlet for Gaul, and consequently a place of considerable commercial activity. Its area was increased by Constantine I from about forty to about forty-five acres.[18] Apparently, the inhabitants of Toulouse who had earlier built four suburbs, now were concentrated within a single circuit wall which enclosed about 240 acres, making it the largest city in southern Gaul.[19] As for Bordeaux, its occupied area was less than one-third of its previous extent, amounting only to some seventy-nine acres, whereas Narbonne comprised a mere thirty-five acres.[20] It seems quite clear that although the restoration of order in Gaul under

Diocletian brought in its wake a certain revival in the towns of Gaul, on the whole they failed to regain their earlier prosperity and population.[21] Many of them suffered further devastation at the hands of the barbarians. In the year 355 forty to forty-five Gallic towns were pillaged by Alemanni, Franks, or Saxons.[22] Energetic and competent rulers such as Constantine I, Julian, and Valentinian I gave the Gallic cities periods of peace which enabled them to repair their damages and to check, or at least to retard, their rate of decline. Even so, the pressure of governmental exactions and bureaucratic misgovernment prevented any permanent recovery. Conditions remained unfavorable for an increase in population, and in the late fourth and fifth centuries the towns of Gaul steadily declined.[23]

For other parts of the Empire in the West information is less definite. Ausonius includes four Spanish cities in his list, but scarcely does more than mention them by name; the *Expositio* does not refer to a single one. The four selected for praise by Ausonius are Seville, Cordova, Tarragon, and Braga.[24] Tarragon, however, does not seem to have recovered from the effects of the disorders of the third century, and Braga's claim to honorable mention is very slight. The once prosperous Carthagina had declined greatly; Barcelona, on the other hand, seems to have acquired greater commercial importance.[25] It is significant of the state of industry in the Spanish cities of the Late Empire that none of the imperial factories was located in any of them, although Spain did export some types of clothing.[26]

Naturally, throughout so large an area as Roman North Africa west of Cyrenaica there was a great deal of diversity in the economic and social conditions of the cities. Carthage continued to be a large city, and many others retained a fair measure of prosperity until the Vandal conquest in the fifth century.[27] Yet some of them had felt the ravages of war in the third century, although by no means to the same extent as had the towns of Gaul.[28] In spite of the fact that during the fourth century the imperial government undertook extensive repairs to public buildings in many communities, some towns remained in a ruined condition.[29] Whether the damage had been caused by military action or was due to neglect on the part of the respective communities, the inability of the towns to carry out the needed restoration by their own efforts implies a condition of impoverishment with an accompanying shortage of manpower. In fact, a serious shrinkage in the number of the higher professional classes by the early fourth century is indicated by the inability of Constantine I to find any architects in the province of Africa.[30] The African cities cannot have failed to suffer from the bitter factional strife of the Donatist schism, complicated as it was by an anti-Roman movement among the impoverished peasantry, as well as from the rebellions and the invasions of semibarbarous peoples which disturbed the country in the course of the fourth century. Caesarea (Cherchel) in Mauretania, which is the one African city besides Carthage mentioned in the *Expositio,* was pillaged and burnt in 372 during the revolt of Firmus.[31] The progressive decline of the agrarian population must, in turn, have affected the population of the urban communities. Virtually no information exists about the state of the towns of Sicily during the Late Empire, but there is no reason to believe that it was any better than that of the cities of Italy to which I shall now turn.

It is the general opinion that the Italian municipalities began to decline in prosperity and population early in the second century.[32] Even if this decline was slow at first, it was certain to become accelerated under the general conditions which prevailed from the time of the Severi. In the fourth century the Italian towns seem in general to have been both smaller and poorer than in the second.[33] Furthermore, the progressive decline in Italian agriculture and the enfeeblement of the rural population afforded them no opportunity of recovery. Rome itself suffered a continuous decline in population. Kahrstedt[34] has estimated that in the fourth century its inhabitants had decreased to 500,000 or 450,000 and in the fifth to 200,000, whereas Lot[35] will not allow that the population exceeded 250,000 in the time of Constantine I. Kahrstedt's figures seem rather generous for the fourth century, and, as was pointed out in the first lecture, any such estimates are at best more or less reasonable calculations, but at any rate they fit in with the over-all view of a declining urban population. The effect on the city of Rome of the general factors operating to produce a decline in population throughout the cities of the western part of the Empire was aggravated by the removal of the imperial court, and with it the central government bureaus, to Milan and later to Ravenna. As might be expected, the decline in Rome was reflected in that of its harbor town, Ostia.[36] Both Milan and Ravenna, in turn, experienced the same sort of boom as Treves in

Gaul with the influx of civil and military personnel. Here is another instance of the shifting of the urban population; there was not necessarily any total increase. Capua, included in the list of Ausonius, owed its selection solely to its old historic importance and not to any contemporary role as a center of industry or commerce.[37] On the other hand, Aquileia, cited both by Ausonius and by the author of the *Expositio,* must have retained a relatively high degree of prosperity. In the Late Empire it occupied a strategic position along what had become the main line of communication between the western and eastern parts of the Empire. It was also the seat of an imperial mint and a weaving plant.[38] Six other towns in North Italy were the sites of imperial arsenals, and there were clothing works at Milan and Ravenna.[39] From this it would seem that the towns of the Po Valley and Venetia were in a much better condition than those of the peninsula, where only Rome, Canusium, and Tarentum had any sort of government factories; even so they were smaller than in medieval times.[40]

From the Danubian provinces and Dalmatia there is no evidence of any general increase in the numbers or prosperity of the urban elements. In fact, Raetia including Vindelicia had never experienced any great amount of urbanization, and this condition remained unchanged after Diocletian. It is true that town life had developed on a much more extensive scale in Noricum under the Principate, but the province suffered very heavily from barbarian inroads during the second, third, and fourth centuries, before its loss to the Empire in the fifth. In the Late Empire there was only one imperial factory in Noricum and that was in the border fortress of Lauriacum on the Danube. Pannonia, like Raetia, was, and remained, a predominantly rural area as well as a frequent battleground in civil and barbarian wars. Its most important city was Sirmium on the lower Save, which is the only one mentioned in the *Expositio*. Sirmium was the site of an arsenal and clothing works, and, owing to its military and administrative importance, may have experienced some growth in the fourth century. Its prosperity, however, declined with its occupation by the Goths in 380. There were other military arsenals at Carnuntum and Aquincum, which, like Lauriacum, were frontier fortresses on the Danube. Siscia on the middle Save had an imperial mint. The only region in this general area which appears to have increased in prosperity, probably with some population increment as well, was the Dalmatian coast. There, Salona and the adjacent Spalato had profited greatly both by their immunity from barbarian attacks and by the favor of the Emperor Diocletian. There was an arsenal at Salona and clothing works at Spalato.[41]

The preceding survey appears to support an interpretation of the demographic history of the cities of the western lands of the Late Roman Empire which would accord with modern theories of urban population trends. Since the rural population kept on diminishing, it was impossible for the towns to make good their numerical losses by drawing in the surrounding village communities. The decrease in the number of imported slaves, combined with a lack of immigration of traders and craftsmen from the eastern part of the

Empire, prevented these losses from being compensated by movements from distant areas. As a result, irrespective of other factors, the urban population was doomed to continue its decline from these causes alone.

I can now proceed to examine the condition of certain classes in the cities whose fortunes during the Late Empire can be followed with enough precision to determine their relation to the general decline of the urban population and the accompanying shortage in manpower. Knowledge of them is derived almost entirely from the *Theodosian Code,* its supplementary *Novellae,* and, to a more limited extent, the *Code of Justinian,* so that, as for the rural population, it can be claimed that we have the official point of view of the imperial government with respect to their condition. First, I shall discuss a number of occupation groups, residing in the city of Rome or elsewhere, upon which the government depended for transporting certain essential foodstuffs to Rome and also for processing and distributing some of these at state cost to a considerable part of the city populace.

It will be recalled that in the Greco-Roman world the governments of the city-states as a rule assumed the responsibility of seeing that there was an adequate supply of essential foods available in the city markets at a reasonable price. Rome was no exception. Its government during both the Republic and the Empire regarded the provisioning of Rome as a matter of cardinal importance. Not only so, but under the Late Republic it adopted the policy of issuing a monthly allowance of free wheat to the poorer citizens residing in Rome itself. The first emperor, Augustus, would not

risk the unpopularity of abolishing this dole, and there-
after the government was saddled with the burden of
supplying free grain to an essentially nonproductive
proletariat numbering about 200,000. To this number
of recipients there came to be added the Praetorian
Guards and the members of the imperial police and
fire brigade of Rome.[42] About the beginning of the
third century the emperor Septimius Severus supplemented the grain dole with an allowance of oil, also at
the expense of the state.[43] Much later in the same century Aurelian (270–75) introduced the practice of
issuing loaves of bread in place of the unmilled wheat,
continued or revived the oil dole, and also provided
for allowances of pork and salt, as well as wine at
reduced price.[44] The distribution of bread in place of
grain and the addition of oil, wine, pork, and salt to
the dole made its administration much more complicated. It cannot be assumed, however, that the cost was
greatly increased. Of course, a larger personnel was
needed to handle the new items and to supervise their
distribution, but, as will be seen, a considerable share
of the additional expense was met by requisitioning the
services of persons engaged in importing or processing
the types of food concerned. Furthermore, there are
good grounds for believing that the population of
Rome had declined noticeably by the time of the Severi
and had been reduced to perhaps less than one-half of
its previous maximum by the time of Aurelian.[45] Under
these conditions, the most logical explanation of the
new and apparently more generous policy of poor relief
initiated by Severus and elaborated by Aurelian is that
members of the proletariat had gradually dwindled to

the point where no serious increase in the imperial budget was needed to defray the expense of the innovations. This is all the more reasonable in view of the general economic decline in the course of the third century and the corresponding falling off in the imperial revenues which would have dissuaded Aurelian, however much he may have wished to increase his popularity in Rome, from making any serious addition to the cost of the administration.

From the beginning of the Early Empire until the close of the dynasty of the Severi in 235 the Roman government apparently was able to find enough shipowners (*navicularii*) in the Mediterranean seaports willing and able, in return for a transport price and other considerations, to carry under voluntary individual contracts the grain destined for the dole to Rome's harbor town at the mouth of the Tiber, and also to bring in cargoes of wheat for general consumption in the capital.[46] It is interesting to note that the considerations referred to began to be added to the contract price as early as the time of Claudius (41–54) and were increased or confirmed under Trajan, Hadrian, Septimius Severus, and Caracalla.[47] The same is true for other persons who were engaged in the provisioning of Rome, such as the millers and bakers (*pistores*), the grain and oil merchants, and the pork dealers.[48] In the municipalities, too, persons practicing trades which enabled them to render essential public services to their communities enjoyed the same favored treatment. The considerations in question consisted for the most part of exemptions from expensive and time-consuming public and private obligations, in particular,

municipal charges on persons and property and guard-
ianships. In Rome these exemptions were accorded
only to such individuals as voluntarily enrolled in the
guilds or colleges made up of persons engaged in common occupations, who as individuals undertook public
contracts. But in some of the municipal colleges, such
as those of the construction workers (*fabri*), enrollment as a member apparently brought with it the obligation to render the required public service and at the
same time the right to enjoy the special privileges
accorded to active members of these organizations.[49]

Under the early emperors the reason for the grants
of special privileges to government contractors was
most probably a desire to make the rewards of public
business more attractive than the profits to be gained
from private contracts or individual enterprise. But
later, under Marcus Aurelius and his successors, it may
well have been that such grants were used for the two-
fold purpose of inducing more persons with the necessary capital to engage in transporting and marketing
food supplies and of keeping up membership in municipal trades guilds, because of the decrease in the
urban population which was beginning to be a matter
of public concern in this period. Nevertheless, until
the beginning of the troubles of the third century, enrollment in the colleges remained voluntary, and the
privileges and immunities were accorded on an individual basis, except as noted above in the case of certain municipal associations of artisans.[50]

The general population loss which the Empire experienced during the troubles of the third century must
have caused a serious decrease in the numbers of those

who served the needs of the food dole in Rome and ministered to the provisioning of the city as a whole. That this was true and that the situation grew worse instead of better is shown all too clearly by the legislation incorporated in the *Theodosian Code* and the *Novellae* of the fifth century. The voluntary element had disappeared completely in the relationship of the members of the colleges with the government. The state now dealt with each college as a single entity and imposed upon it an obligation in the form of transportation, preparation, or distribution of foods of various kinds, but the colleges had to be strong enough both numerically and financially in order to perform their allotted functions. Accordingly, the state tried to maintain the finances of the colleges by forbidding any of their members to withdraw the capital that they had invested in the businesses in which they engaged as members of the respective associations. This obligation imposed on capital passed from one generation to the next, for all those who inherited property that was so obligated had to allow it to remain in the business concerned. But capital without personnel to employ it properly could not serve the needs of the government; therefore, the emperors ruled that once a man had been enrolled in a college or "corporation" (a term which came into common use for the guilds or colleges in the Late Empire), he must continue to be an active member of it as long as he lived, unless excused for some special reason. Furthermore, because in view of the general decline in population the corporations could not be recruited by voluntary enrollment from outside and because the demands of the state discouraged the children of members from entering them, the government made it obligatory for such children upon coming of age to enroll in their parents' corporations and to carry on the appropriate occupations. Thus, the members of the corporations engaged in the provisioning of Rome were transformed into hereditary occupation groups similar to those of the agricultural workers.[51] Let me cite some of the evidence.

In the *Theodosian Code* thirty-eight constitutions dating from 314 to 414 are devoted to the shipowners (*navicularii*).[52] These show that as early as 314 a *navicularius* was considered to be born into his profession.[53] In other words, his status was already hereditary, and he must enter and remain in his father's corporation, although the obligation had to be reaffirmed in 390.[54] The property of shipowners when invested in this business became permanently attached thereto, as is revealed by a law of 315.[55] Anyone who received such property by inheritance, even if not a shipowner, found that it was bound to the service of shipping and could not be put to other uses. A number of constitutions reiterate the long-standing exemptions from local municipal services which the *navicularii* had received in the past. At times it is stated expressly that these privileges had been granted so that their capital might not be diminished by other demands upon it,[56] but in some cases it is clear that the government was also concerned that the individual *navicularius* remain free from other time-consuming activities that might interfere with the performance of his transport obligations.[57] In other words, the general shortage of eligible persons in the municipalities continually tempted both local and imperial officials to disregard the orders of the emperors and to draft shipowners and their properties for the performance of other duties. But there were not enough *navicularii* enrolled in corporations to permit them to spend their time holding municipal offices or to be subjected to any interference from other sources. How serious the scarcity of shipowners had become by the second half of the fourth century is revealed by a constitution of 371, which ordered the drafting of suitable persons into the corporation of those residing in the eastern provinces.[58]

Until well into the fifth century the millers and bakers formed a single guild in Rome, for the bakers ground their own wheat into flour. Only after the introduction of water-powered flour mills into the city did they come to be organized into two distinct corporations. The *Theodosian Code* and the *Novellae* recognize no distinction between the two occupations and use the term *pistores* in its former two-fold meaning.[59] These millers and bakers were persons of property, the owners and managers of the mills and bakeries, and not the actual workmen, who were slaves. By the time of Constantine I the Roman bakers had become hereditary members of their corporation.[60] Their capital in the form of buildings and equipment could not be freely disposed of but had to remain invested in the baking business. In fact, anyone who acquired a baker's property by inheritance or otherwise had either to enroll and become active in the bakers' corporation or surrender the property in question to it.[61] A serious shortage of personnel among the bakers is attested not only by their hereditary status but also by the practice of forcibly enrolling among them delinquent officials and other persons not already bound to a hereditary service.[62] Furthermore, if the daughter of a miller married someone outside the corporation, her husband was compelled to join it and become bound to it just as if he had inherited this status.[63] The bakers also suffered continually from a shortage of slave labor. In order to remedy this, Constantine I and later emperors assigned to the service of the bakers' corporation in Rome persons who were condemned to slavery for certain types of crime not only in Rome and Italy but even in the provinces.[64]

Other corporations associated with the grain supply of Rome also were faced with a declining membership and consequently were transformed into fixed, hereditary groups. But since their descendants were not numerous enough to keep up the membership to the required strength, the state resorted to conscription to make good the deficit. For example, freedmen in Rome who acquired by gift or testament property that was not liable to the services of the bakers' corporation found themselves perforce assigned to that of the pack drivers who were engaged in transporting grain from Ostia to Rome.[65] Nor was the situation of the meat dealers any different. In 334 the corporation of the swine merchants had shrunk to a mere handful of persons, and anyone who accepted capital invested in this business had to become a member of the association.[66] It goes without saying that membership in this corporation was hereditary and that once an individual was entered on its rolls he could not be released from its obligations. Not only so, but those who took refuge in flight were recalled to their duty if they were de-tected.[67] This tendency to abscond became particularly marked at the end of the fourth and the beginning of the fifth century, as is attested by constitutions of 389, 397, and 408, issued in the hope of checking the desertions.[68] The beef and mutton dealers (*boarii* and *pecuarii*) had likewise come to be bound to hereditary corporations together with their invested capital.[69] And the same seems to have been true of the wine and oil handlers.[70] As has been seen, the hereditary status of these corporations was established by the time of Constantine I. It is not certain, however, what earlier emperor or emperors were responsible for creating it. On this point the sources are completely silent. It is possible that Aurelian found it necessary to resort to this measure in order to ensure the manpower necessary for his expanded system of poor relief. It is more likely, however, that Diocletian took the step in connection with his wide-reaching fiscal innovations. In the early fifth century the state corporations of Rome were suffering from attempts by their members to escape from the city, and the Emperor Honorius had to order the recovery of such fugitives.[71] But enough for the city of Rome. I shall now turn to the municipalities of Italy and the western provinces.

Like the merchants and artisans of Rome, those living in the municipalities, with some exceptions to be noted later, by the latter part of the third century had been organized in colleges that were under government control. In the Late Empire their condition was similar to that of the corporations of Rome which were not engaged in the provisioning of that city. Unlike the shipowners and bakers, they did not have to devote all their time to executing government commissions, but from time to time their personnel and resources were requisitioned for the performance of public services for their municipalities or for the central administration.[72] It can safely be assumed that this class of persons suffered a very serious loss in members as a result of the general decline in the urban population from the late second century and more especially during the years 235 to 284. The archaeological evidence from Gaul in particular seems to indicate an almost complete disappearance of the industrial elements in the cities and a great decrease among those engaged in trade and transportation.[73] This does not mean, however, that in Gaul industry and commerce came to a complete standstill. Luxury goods, such as glassware, continued to be manufactured or imported in considerable quantities and there was also a sizable output of Gallic clothing of various sorts. A good deal of the latter, however, as well as other articles of necessity, probably was produced at the villas of the great landholders by their dependent workers. In general, a similar condition seems to have prevailed, although to varying extent, in Italy and the other western areas, for the general meagerness of the inscriptional evidence points to a great decline in the activities and prosperity of the commercial and industrial guilds. In Roman economic life a decrease in prosperity was intimately related to a falling off in the number of persons engaged in production and distribution. The legislation of the Late Empire affecting the municipal corporations is not nearly so extensive or illuminating as that regarding the groups which served the food supply of the city of Rome. But such as it is, it shows that the imperial government had to face a similar problem in maintaining the strength of these colleges and dealt with it in a similar fashion.

Every municipal corporation was obligated to some sort of public service, one which corresponded to the occupation of its members. Consequently, each had its special role to play in the life of its municipality. Because of this and because local commerce and industry depended upon the activities of the corporations, the government felt it essential that they be kept alive. Another important reason for this solicitude on the part of the state was that the performance of certain public obligatory services by the corporations spared it the necessity of expanding the number of its local officials with a proportionate increase in government expenses. And at the same time the members of the corporations were a direct source of revenue, for, although exempt from the property tax, they were subject to a trade tax known as the *chrysargyrium* or "gold and silver tax" because it had to be paid in coin and not in kind.[74] Each corporation carried out its obligatory duties under the direction of its town council, whether the service was rendered to the municipality alone or to the imperial government. The best known of the municipal guilds are those of the *fabri*, who comprised the building trades; the *centonarii*, makers of patchwork mats and hangings; and the *dendrofori*, woodsmen. Together, these three corporations had the duty of serving as the municipal fire brigades.[75] In the earliest laws of the *Theodosian Code*, which, as has

been seen, date from the time of Constantine I, these
corporations appear as both obligatory and hereditary
bodies.[76] The properties of the members are likewise
bound in perpetuity to the professional activities of the
corporations.[77] Further evidence of a continued or
growing shortage of manpower in some of the corporations early in the fourth century is found in a law of
Constantine I which ordered that all colleges of *dendrofori* be united with those of the *centonarii* and the
construction workers, since these groups needed to be
strengthened by a great number of men.[78] The ranks
of these corporations continued to be depleted in the
course of the fourth century. As a result, the public
burdens resting upon the remainder became propor-
tionately heavier, and they took to flight to escape the
intolerable load. In 397 an imperial constitution ordered the recovery of all deserters from the municipal
corporations.[79] In 400 the Emperor Honorius complained of the very great numbers of *corporati* who
were deserting the cities to lose themselves as *coloni*
in the rural areas, thus contributing to the ruin of their
cities.[80] Up to the last days of the Western Empire its
rulers continued to fight a losing battle to maintain
the membership of these associations at a level sufficiently high to enable them to perform the public services to which they were liable.[81]

At this point I should like to consider briefly some
elements in the population of the cities which remained
outside the obligatory corporations. These comprised
the professional classes, the artists, and the artisans
who practiced highly specialized crafts which were
regarded as most desirable but not essential to the eco-

nomic life of the municipalities or the state. These were teachers, doctors, architects, and those who designed and executed works of art of all sorts. As might be expected, there are few references to these groups in the legislation of the fourth and fifth centuries. Such as there are, however, do seem to indicate concern on the part of the government about the scarcity of qualified persons in these activities. I have already had occasion to refer to the constitution of 334 in which Constantine I declared that there were no architects available in the African provinces and proceeded to offer inducements to young men to undergo the necessary training.[82] In 337 the same emperor exempted members of thirty-seven professions and trades from all public municipal services, which is another indication of a lack of adequate numbers in these occupations and of an attempt to overcome it.[83] Special exemptions from obligations of this sort and also from taxation were granted to professors and physicians.[84] This indulgence may also be interpreted as due in part, at least, to a similar shortage of personnel. But any such attempts to increase the numbers in these professional groups must have been futile in view of the general decline in the urban population. In addition, the restrictions placed upon the sons of municipal councilors, who would have been the natural recruits for the learned professions, and upon the children of the *corporati,* from whose ranks the craftsmen might be expected to come, eliminated any possibility of filling up their rolls from these sources.

Less fortunate was the lot of some other occupation groups which contributed in various ways to the entertainment of the urban population both in Rome and in the municipalities of the Western Empire. These were the actors and actresses of all kinds, the charioteers who competed in the races in the circuses or hippodromes, the fortune tellers, the image bearers, and the banner carriers, who were in demand at the celebration of games and festivals of pagan origin. In the fourth century the numbers of these persons decreased along with those of the other urban elements, although the popular demand for amusement at the public expense continued unabated, and the emperors did not venture to ignore it.[85] Consequently, these groups of professional entertainers were treated like the businessmen and artisans whose services appeared essential to the public interest. They were organized in corporations or at least were registered on official lists, their occupations were made hereditary, they were forbidden to engage in any other professions or to marry outside of their groups, and they were prohibited from leaving the cities in which they were enrolled. Toward the close of the fourth century and in the early fifth, their numbers must have become seriously depleted, to judge from the ordinances which were issued to prevent them from escaping their hereditary obligations.[86]

Finally, I shall now take up an element in the urban population about which there is very considerable information. This is the class of the *curiales,* or town councilors, who formed a special economic as well as political group in the cities of the Empire, with the exception of Rome and Constantinople. They might be called the municipal senatorial order. In the Early Empire this group was composed of business men and the middle-class landholders who resided in the cities. They formed the bourgeoisie of the Empire and controlled the government of the Italian and provincial towns in which they were the backbone of the economic life and the leaders in cultural progress. From their ranks were elected the municipal magistrates and the town councilors. At their own expense these officials carried the burden of local government, and gladly and proudly provided both useful and ornamental public works and established endowments for the benefit of their fellow citizens.[87] By the early third century, however, the municipal bourgeoisie was in a state of economic decline. It is well known that Septimius Severus had imposed on the municipal councils the responsibility for collecting taxes due the state from the residents of the municipalities and the territories under their administrative control. The various expenses and penalties involved in the discharge of this obligation proved too heavy a burden for the local senatorial order to bear. Eligible persons showed unwillingness to present themselves as candidates for public office, and hence the councils had to resort to compulsory nominations. Office holders no longer found themselves in a position to carry on their inherited tradition of public munificence. There was a rapid falling off both of their gifts to the cities and of the inscriptions in which they had proudly recorded their public careers.[88]

Not only did the bourgeoisie suffer an economic decline, they also declined in numbers. This numerical shrinkage is what should be expected, since such a decrease was common to urban centers in general, and furthermore this was one of the classes in the Roman world the members of which deliberately limited the size of their families or preferred to remain childless. With the rural population and the other urban elements already declining in prosperity and numbers, the bourgeoisie could find no replacements from these natural sources of recruitment. Confirmation of this condition comes in the passage of Ulpian previously cited which reveals that, owing to the scarcity of eligible persons among the propertied class, the town councils had resorted to the appointment of minors to municipal offices.[89] The disorders of the third century inevitably led to a further decrease both in numbers and in wealth of the municipal senatorial order. In Gaul, for example, the prosperous municipal business class seems to have disappeared,[90] a situation which appears to have been true generally throughout the West. For when a fair amount of order was re-established in the late third century, the class of the *curiales* was made up almost entirely of small proprietors who owned a minimum of twenty-five *iugera* (between eighteen and nineteen acres) of cultivated land. Few of them appear to have engaged in business enterprises.[91]

The *curiales* [92] formed an essential cog in the administrative machinery of the Late Empire. As under the Principate, in each city they constituted the municipal council, which was not only responsible for carrying on local government but had also to play the role of an agent of the imperial bureaucracy. Every municipal councilor was obliged to fill in his turn each of the local public offices. As municipal officials the *curiales* collected and disbursed city revenues, saw to the local food supply, operated the public baths, provided spectacles of various kinds for public entertainment, and maintained municipal public works. In addition, they had to take turns in holding the various official posts through which the council fulfilled its responsibilities to the state. As representatives of the council in these capacities, they assigned and raised the state taxes in money and in kind, collected and transported military supplies, saw to the provisioning of troops in transit, furnished relays for the public post, and carried out the orders of imperial officials in other matters. In the performance of some of these duties the councilors could command the services of the municipal corporations; in others they disbursed civic or state funds, but they themselves served without salaries, received no compensation for their activities, and had to defray many necessary expenditures out of their own resources. Not only so, but the *curiales* as a group in each city were forced to go surety with their properties for the full collection of the imperial taxes and imposts, a responsibility which fell first of all upon those who happened to be in office during any given year. In view of this wide range of functions and responsibilities it is quite understandable that the Emperor Majorian said: "No one is unaware that the *curiales* are the nerves of the state and the vital organs of the cities." [93] The government of the Late Empire had every reason to be concerned about the maintenance of their numbers and of their solvency.

That such was the case is amply attested by the 192 laws which successive emperors issued with respect to the *curiales* between 313 and 436.[94] In the earliest of these constitutions it is implied that the *curialis* was bound to his *curia* or council just as the *colonus* was bound to an estate and the craftsman to his corporation.[95] Others of slightly later date show that this status was hereditary, and that a *curialis* might only be released from it when he had filled all of the municipal offices and performed the other obligatory services to which councilors were liable.[96] Needless to say, the property of the councilors was assigned in perpetuity to finance the performance of the personal and property services which rested upon them through their *curiae*.[97] These early fourth-century laws date from the reign of Constantine I, but that emperor was not responsible for creating the permanent and hereditary condition of the *curiales*. By his time their status had become definitely fixed, and it must have been so from the time of Diocletian. As with the other groups which have been considered so far, this is a clear indication that the *curiales* as a class emerged from the troubles of the third century so weakened numerically that the government was faced with a shortage of personnel for carrying on local administration and enforcing the demands which it laid upon its subjects.

Nor did this condition improve in the course of the fourth and fifth centuries. In a constitution of 326 Constantine I complained that the councils were being left desolate.[98] Desperate attempts were made by various emperors to find replacements from other groups. Sons of civil servants who declined to follow their fathers' careers were assigned to the councils from 329, and from 341 the sons of soldiers who were unfit to bear arms were also forcibly enrolled among the *curiales* because of "scarcity of men." [99] In view of the burdens which the state imposed upon the municipal councilors individually and collectively, it is no wonder that so many of them tried to desert their councils and their cities. Many, in despair, simply took to the forests or the deserts. More sought to evade their hereditary status by entering the civil and military services, by enrolling in monastic communities, by becoming tenants of great landholders, or by taking refuge among the professional corporations. Like those who were bound to other hereditary occupation castes, they were excluded by law from these would-be havens of refuge and, if detected therein, they were dragged back to their original councils.[100] An exception was made in favor of those who wished to enter the regular clergy, provided that they found substitutes to take their places or ceded their properties to the group of *curiales* which they were leaving.[101] Even if, after completing the full series of their obligations, any *curiales* attained the rank of senator and consequently were emancipated from their inherited condition, their children born before this emancipation were assigned to their fathers' *curiae*.[102] Granted, however, that a fair number of runaways managed to escape detection, this does not furnish the basic explanation of the steady decline in the numbers of the *curiales*. A far more influential factor was their progressive impoverishment caused by the expenses involved in the performance of their duties, the oppression of the corrupt and avaricious government officials under whom they served, and their indebtedness to their wealthier neighbors. Those whose properties shrank below the minimum requirement of their class had to be dropped from its rolls. Those who did manage to retain enough property to remain in the *curiae* were no longer either able or willing to raise families large enough to replace the numerical losses of their order. So notorious was the shortage of *curiales* in the third quarter of the fourth century that when the Emperor Valentinian ordered the execution of three of them in each of a group of towns, Florentius, the prefect of Gaul, dared to ask, "What is to be done if there are not so many in any town?" [103] And the complaint of Majorian in 458 about the ruin of the senatorial order in the cities shows only too clearly that in the next century the shortage had become even more acute.[104]

I have, I trust, been able to produce specific evidence of manpower deficiency among the merchants, traders, craftsmen, and urban landholders of the cities in the western part of the Roman world during the Late Empire. This amply confirms the view of an initial numerical deficiency and a progressive downward trend in the urban population of this period, which was deduced from other, more general, considerations.

IV

The Government Services

HAVING EXAMINED the evidence for a shortage of manpower in the agrarian population of the Roman Empire in the West and also in certain major categories of the inhabitants of the cities, I now propose to survey the government services of the Late Empire in order to see if the information available about them gives any indication of a similar shortage of personnel. In "government services" I include the military service, the civil service, and the employees in the government factories and other state enterprises.

Under military service I shall discuss the army alone because information regarding the navy of the Late Empire is too inadequate for any conclusion to be drawn about its strength or problems of recruitment. It is necessary first of all to form an estimate of the actual size of the army, both because there is some basis for making a rough estimate and because its size has an important bearing on the problem of its recruitment from the population of the Empire as a whole. It should be remembered that from the time of Augustus the army of the Roman Empire was a professional army, in which the soldiers spent a major part of their lives and which, in theory at least, was maintained continuously at full strength. Since there was no system of reserves or a national militia to back up the standing army, I do not need to discuss troops of these types.

The first problem is to estimate the size of the army at the accession of Diocletian in 284. Since historical sources contain no definite statement on this point, all calculations must be based on what is known about the army of the Early Empire and changes that it underwent during the period 235 to 284. At the accession of Septimius Severus in 193 there were thirty legions composed of soldiers who were Roman citizens. Severus increased these by three, and Alexander Severus added another, making a total of thirty-four legions by 235.[1] Since the full strength of each legion was approximately 6,000 men, the total number of legionaries should have been about 204,000. In addition to these there were the so-called auxiliaries, smaller detachments of infantry and cavalry recruited from non-Roman elements in the Roman provinces or among client peoples outside the frontiers. With the extension of Roman citizenship in 212 to practically all free inhabitants of the Empire, the provincial auxiliaries became citizen soldiers like the legionaries, but the status of the foreign corps remained unchanged. It must be admitted that information concerning the number of the auxiliary troops in 235 is very uncertain.

In the time of Augustus there were about 150,000, a number equal to that of the twenty-five legions in service in 14. According to Tacitus this was not a constant relationship because the number of auxiliary units varied from time to time.[2] By the middle of the second century they had been increased to about 200,000.[3] If this was the number still in service in 193, the total in the thirty legions and the auxiliary units was some 380,000. Yet most modern authorities are inclined to scale this down to 300,000 or fewer, allowing, apparently, for reductions among the auxiliaries.[4] If the four legions organized between 193 and 235 are added, the total was about 400,000, unless it is admitted that the auxiliaries were deliberately decreased as the number of the legions rose. This figure does find support in some quarters although the general tendency is to accept 300,000 as the strength of the army in 235, irrespective of the Praetorian Guard and other military units in Rome.[5] Five new legions were added between 235 and 284, making a total of thirty-nine, and there were also new formations of other troops,[6] but it is uncertain how many of the auxiliary corps disappeared during the wars of this period. Yet it seems safe to assume a total increase,[7] and I find myself in agreement with those who allow about 400,000 for the size of the army at the accession of Diocletian.[8] The number is of importance because it must be used in estimating the size of the new levies made by that emperor and his successors.

Under Diocletian and Constantine I the Roman army was both enlarged and reorganized. It came to be divided into two groups: the field troops (*palatini* and *comitatenses*) and the frontier guards (*limitanei, riparienses*). The army of the Late Empire must be regarded as the joint product of both, although Diocletian appears to have done more to increase the number of troops and Constantine to have contributed more in separating the field army from that of the frontiers.[9] I am not so much concerned here with the categories of troops as with the size of this new army. On this point some statements have been made by writers of the period, but unfortunately they cannot be accepted at their face value. The Christian writer Lactantius says of Diocletian: "For he appointed three partners in his authority, the world being divided into four parts and the armies multiplied, since each of them strove to have a far greater number of soldiers than the earlier emperors had had when they governed the state alone." [10] This passage has been interpreted as a statement to the effect that Diocletian quadrupled the size of the army, and in that sense has properly been rejected as an absurd exaggeration.[11] But it is unnecessary to take Lactantius literally here, particularly in view of his following statement: "Indeed, the number of those receiving [pay] had begun to be greater than that of those who paid [taxes]."

The sixth-century writer Lydus has left a statement that Diocletian had an army of 389,704 and a navy of 45,000, both of which were doubled by Constantine.[12] Since, in fact, it was Diocletian rather than Constantine who was responsible for the bulk of the increase in the number of troops, Lydus' army of 780,-000 must be regarded as largely imaginary. He may have been misled by the separation of the field and border troops completed under Constantine, which he interpreted as a doubling of the original army.[13] The figure given by Lydus, however, would seem to rest upon some definite information since it is in exact and not in round numbers. It could refer to the strength of Diocletian's army at the beginning or the close of his reign.[14] A fifth-century historian, Zosimus, states that the troops under the command of Constantine in 312 were about 100,000 strong.[15] If that is an all-inclusive figure, it means that each of the four emperors had an army of about that size and that the army as a whole numbered about 400,000. If, however, it referred only to field troops exclusive of border garrisons, the total was much higher.[16] This latter possibility, however, appears less likely in view of estimates of the size of the field army, which will be given later.

Another historian, Agathias, writing in the sixth century, contrasts the strength of the military establishment before the division of the Empire in 395 with that of his own time and gives the former as 645,000 men.[17] This does not seem to be an impossible figure, although doubtless it represents an authorized rather than an effective strength. Finally, there is the evidence of the *Notitia Dignitatum,* which in its present form probably dates from 435 at the latest. This document gives a list of the military units under the command of the general officers of both field and garrison troops. Consequently, one might expect to be able to use it as a reliable basis for calculating the strength of the imperial army in the fourth and fifth centuries. Unfortunately, however, the *Notitia* is incomplete for some of the western provinces, and in one instance at least its data apply to the third century and not even approximately to the time of its final compilation. For these reasons there is general agreement that although it may be used with safety in computing the strength of the field army in the fourth century, it cannot be relied upon for an estimate of the frontier garrisons, particularly in the western part of the Empire.[18] It is also agreed that by the close of the fourth century the army units were not maintained at full strength.[19] Mommsen made a tentative calculation of the size of the army of the *Notitia* at 554,500 without the border troops in Italy, Gaul, Britain, and North Africa, whereas Nischer computed a total paper strength of 737,500. As Delbrück has pointed out, any such figures are absurd for the early fifth century.[20]

Modern writers have tried to calculate the size of the army of Diocletian and Constantine from the number of the new infantry and cavalry units created by them, but this method is not completely satisfactory, since the origin of many formations is in doubt, as is also the strength of certain corps. For example, it is safe to accept an increase of about twenty legions under Diocletian, but that does not mean an increase in personnel of 50 per cent because it is not known how many new legions were recruited to the same strength as the old, how many were formed of detachments from the latter, or how many were created by new levies. Certainly, many new cavalry units were formed by mounted troops detached from the legions, and Constantine increased his field forces by withdrawing units from the frontier garrisons.[21] Accordingly, in view of the lack of dependable statistics, modern calculations of the army strength after the reorganization under Diocletian and Constantine must be expected to vary and must be looked upon merely as more or less reasonable estimates. It seems fairly certain, however, that no important increases in the military establishment occurred in the course of the late fourth or fifth centuries.[22] Some representative computations of the size of the army in the fourth century will now be considered. The lowest figure is that of Piganiol, less than 400,000;[23] Seeck prefers 400,000, but admits the possibility of 600,000;[24] Lot estimates the number between 450,000 and 471,000;[25] Cary, Grosse, Stein, and Segrè are in close agreement at about 500,000;[26] and the highest total is that of J. B. Bury, 600,000 to 650,000.[27] In all of these totals there is a constant factor, namely, the size of the field army, which is placed at about 200,000;[28] the variable is the number allowed for the border garrisons. In the light of the foregoing discussion, I favor approximately 500,000 if the army mustered 350,000 in 284; 550,000 if it was then about 400,000, which in either case amounts to an increase of 150,000 at most.

The question may now be asked: What effect did the recruitment of about 150,000 new troops have upon the manpower of the Empire and in particular upon its western half? Did the recruitment, as has recently been suggested, of itself produce such a critical shortage among the rural population that its presumed recovery from the losses of the period 235–84 was checked and instead was turned into a decline under pressure of government exactions and regimentation?[29] Since the mobile forces stationed in the East and the West were approximately equal, although the frontier garrisons of the former were considerably larger than those of the latter, it may be assumed that the West bore a lighter load than the East in meeting the new levies.[30] Accordingly, the West would be called upon to furnish fewer than 75,000 new troops, perhaps not more than 50,000. Furthermore, the raising of the new levies was spread over a considerable number of years. Undoubtedly, most of the new units were organized between 285 and 305, but certainly a fair number were created after 312.[31]

The full burden of supplying the required numbers, however, did not fall upon the rural inhabitants of the Empire. Very many of the new troops were drawn from its barbarian neighbors. As has been seen, the practice of recruiting barbarians was well established before Diocletian's accession. One of his immediate predecessors, Probus, had not been content to accept recruits from barbarians settled on Roman soil, but had introduced others from without the Empire directly into Roman corps. Diocletian himself was responsible for planting fresh colonies of barbarians in the West with the obligation that they furnish soldiers, and seems to have been very ready to accept money payments in place of Roman recruits so that he could hire volunteers, of whom the majority would naturally be foreigners.[32] Constantine resorted even more freely to enrolling Germans in his new corps.[33] Of course, it is impossible to determine what proportion of the recruits was barbarian, but if one quarter of them were non-Roman, which does not seem unreasonable, the older agrarian population in the West would have had to furnish only about 40,000 men in addition to the regular replacements for the corps already in existence. Surely that would not have proved to be such a crushing burden, as has sometimes been maintained,[34] if the rural population had been on the upswing. If, on the other hand, as I hope I have demonstrated was more probably the case, the rural population of the Empire had not begun to recover from the decline which had set in by the opening of the third century, but was still in process of recession, then the rate of decrease might have been somewhat accelerated and agricultural production would also have decreased because of an increased shortage of manpower. That such was the situation may be reflected in the complaint raised by Lactantius about the cost of maintaining the military and civil service as enlarged by Diocletian.[35] The very fact that Diocletian did resort to planting barbarians within the Empire for both military and fiscal reasons confirms the view that the surviving rural population was too small to meet the demands made upon it even before that emperor carried through his military reforms.

Following the example of their predecessors the rulers of the Late Empire endeavored to maintain the strength of their army by a regular system of recruitment. It will be recalled that the troops were professional soldiers. Those enrolled in the field units served for twenty years, those in the frontier garrisons for twenty-five years unless they were incapacitated earlier. It has been calculated that the legionaries in the army of the Early Empire, whose term of service was twenty years, required a normal annual replacement of 20 per cent.[36] Since the field troops of the Late Empire had at their maximum a strength of 194,500, they needed, at the same replacement rate, about 40,000 recruits each year. If a total of roughly 550,000 is accepted for the army as a whole, about 350,000 must be allowed for the border troops. If their twenty-five year term of service is taken into account, they would have had to receive replacements at the rate of 16 per cent annually, or about 56,000 men. This would mean finding some 96,000 recruits annually for the army as a whole. Some years would have passed, however, before the new units organized under Diocletian and his successors needed replacements at the same rate as the older corps. At the most, the quota for the western half of the Empire, comprising Britain, Gaul and the Rhineland, Spain, North Africa except Libya and Egypt, Italy with its adjacent islands, and the provinces of the upper and middle Danube, would have reached considerably less than 48,000 per year even on the assumption that the units were maintained at strength, which was by no means the case.[37] If any serious difficulties were encountered in raising that number, they must have been due in large measure to a shortage of available manpower. And there is dependable evidence that such difficulties not only did exist, but kept on increasing throughout the fourth and early fifth centuries.

Shortage of manpower offers the best explanation of the methods of recruitment employed in the Late Empire.[38] Although theoretically the old universal liability to military service still existed for all male Roman citizens who reached the age of eighteen years, it was rarely enforced and then only within limited areas. This practice was a legacy from the Early Empire, but a rather obvious reason why it could not be changed and a more general use made of the principle of universal liability was the already existing shortage of personnel in agriculture, industry, transportation, and municipal services. The government simply could not risk withdrawing too many persons from these occupations. Only upon men who had no steady occupation (*vagi*) and those who did not belong to the groups with hereditary status (*otiosi* or *vacantes*) was the draft enforced as far as possible. Diocletian, however, imposed a modified form of draft upon rural landholdings. Under this system the agricultural land was divided in units (*capitula*) of fixed size, and one recruit had to be furnished every year for each such unit. If a landholder possessed several units, he was required to furnish a corresponding number of recruits from his dependents; if he had only a fraction of a unit, his land was combined with that of his neighbors to make up a full unit for which they were jointly responsible. In place of recruits the government could call upon the landholders to contribute sums of money to be used in hiring volunteers.

Another evidence of difficulty in finding recruits is seen in the imposition upon the sons of soldiers and veterans of a hereditary obligation to enlist. Certainly from the time of Diocletian, and possibly earlier, the sons of veterans had to present themselves as recruits upon reaching the proper age.[39] The same was true of the sons of soldiers in active service. Even before they became old enough to bear arms, they were entered on the rolls of the corps to which their fathers belonged.[40] Only those who failed to meet the required physical standards were excused from military service and, as has been pointed out, were assigned to the class of the *curiales* in the appropriate municipality. The border garrisons came to have a status closely resembling that of the *coloni* and *corporati*. They were assigned lands to cultivate in the neighborhood of the forts to which they were attached. The crops which they raised contributed to their support and consequently they received smaller allowances than the field troops. Thus, they had the two-fold hereditary obligation of tilling the soil and rendering military service.[41]

Since the number of recruits provided by rural proprietorships and the families of soldiers proved inadequate, Diocletian and his successors continued the already established practice of planting groups of barbarians on the vacant lands of the Empire with the dual purpose of keeping the land under cultivation so that it could pay the tax in kind and of providing new manpower resources for the army. These groups were organized as hereditary corporations, each obligated to supply a fixed annual quota of recruits.[42] The history of this form of colonization indicates clearly that its military objective was far more important than its fiscal in the eyes of the government. In addition to the quotas supplied by these groups of foreigners, the emperors resorted to the direct recruitment of barbarian volunteers from without the Empire. Prisoners of war were given the opportunity to enlist in various military units,[43] and furthermore there was a ready reception accorded to individual barbarians who crossed the frontier to enter the service of Rome. It cannot be imagined that the imperial government was unaware of the dangers inherent in an ever-increasing proportion of barbarians both in the rank and file and in the officer corps of the Roman armies. If, then, the government felt obliged to rely more and more upon non-Roman elements in order to provide for the defense of the Empire, this can hardly have resulted from any other cause than the increasing lack of available reserves among the Romans themselves.[44]

That such was the case is confirmed in part by the frequency of the imperial edicts dealing with the sons of soldiers and veterans who sought to avoid their inherited obligation to military service. Between 319 and 398 no fewer than twenty-two such laws were promulgated, a sufficient indication that there was a general tendency for members of this class to shirk their duty and at the same time a desperate need on the part of the state for their services.[45] Further proof of the difficulty in finding recruits lies in the change of the government's attitude towards the enlistment of slaves. It had long been a fundamental principle of Roman public law that slaves should not be admitted to the ranks of the army. In the Late Empire they formed the only class of persons who remained automatically disqualified for military service, but the need for recruits became so pressing that by the late fourth century slaves could be accepted under special circumstances. When this happened, of course they received their freedom upon enrollment. In the desperate conditions of the year 406 the Emperor Honorius actually issued a general call for slaves in the western provinces to enlist alongside the free population.[46] It was, furthermore, a matter of government policy to exempt the imperial domains from furnishing recruits like other, private, estates. On more than one occasion, however, this exemption had to be withdrawn and the imperial tenants made liable to military service.[47] The shortage of eligible recruits is reflected also in a law of 367 which reduced the minimum height requirement for Italian recruits for the field army units from about five feet eight inches to about five feet five inches in order to obtain the necessary replacements.[48] The physical standards for the border garrisons also could not be maintained at the level required for the mobile forces.

It may seem contradictory in the face of the evidence presented with regard to manpower shortage in so many elements of the population to find it generally agreed among modern scholars that the majority of the recruits for the field units, at least, were secured by voluntary enlistment.[49] In this connection, however, the term "voluntary" is used in a very broad sense. It is made to include prisoners of war who elected to join the Roman army rather than suffer a worse fate, as well as the mercenaries who were recruited among the barbarians beyond the frontiers. In addition, those members of the corporate groups of barbarian colonists bound to furnish an annual quota of recruits who presented themselves to the recruiting officers of their own accord can likewise be classed as volunteers, but it must be admitted that many Romans enlisted voluntarily because of the substantial advantages which the soldier enjoyed over the ordinary civilian. Among these advantages were the right to defend oneself against all charges in a military court, immunity from all municipal services, and generous exemptions from taxation. In 370 the emperors Valentinian and Valens sought to entice more volunteers by granting freedom from taxation to soldiers and their wives after the former had completed five years in the service. Five years later they extended this immunity to the parents of field troops.[50] But, one may ask, where did the Roman volunteers come from? They came partly, of course, from those classes of the population which were not bound by hereditary obligation to serve some particular occupation group, but also in large measure from men belonging to the classes of *coloni, curiales,* and *corporati,* who fled from their hereditary groups in the hope of finding a less intolerable form of life. Unless a substantial number of these fugitives had found their way into the ranks of the army, there would have been no need for the repeated orders of the emperors that they be forcibly recalled to their original status. In fact, Valentinian and Valens found it advisable to grant personal immunity from the obligations of their class to the *curiales* who had managed to get into the army and remain in active service for five years.[51] The preference for volunteers is to be explained both on the ground that they were considered to have greater aptitude for military life than conscripts, and also because the quality of the recruits obtained under the system of levies on the land units described above was very inferior.

If still further evidence is needed to show that the army of the Late Empire suffered from a continual shortage of manpower, it is to be found in the fact that the units of the field army, the elite corps in the military establishment, could not be maintained at full strength. Special levies had to be resorted to in putting the army on a war footing for major campaigns.[52] All modern authorities are agreed that by the fifth century the army of the Western Empire as revealed in the *Notitia Dignitatum* was nothing but an army on paper whose strength bore no relation to the effectives that were actually at the disposal of the government.[53] It is likewise agreed that by this time the garrison troops had sunk to the status of a border militia virtually without any military value. The inability of the imperial government to keep its forces up to nominal strength is the main reason why the Roman armies were so small in important campaigns. Against the Alemanni at Strassburg in 357 the Caesar Julian had only 13,000 men under his command, and in the critical battle of Hadrianople in 378 the army of the Emperor Valens was no larger.[54] The feeble resistance offered by the Western Empire to the invasions of the Visigoths, Alans, Suevi, Vandals, and Burgundians, whose actual fighting strength was surprisingly small, finds its chief explanation in the even greater numerical weakness of the Romans themselves.[55] There can be no doubt that the financial difficulties of the administration were to a large extent, although not primarily, responsible for the collapse of the military establishment. The emperors were able to pay very substantial subsidies to their barbarian allies, which could have been spent to far greater advantage in maintaining the strength of the Roman armies, had this been possible. The Romans of the Late Empire would then have turned back the barbarian invasions, as the Romans of the Republic and of the Early Empire had succeeded in doing.

Next to be considered is the imperial civil service, the employees of which formed a large and important element in the population.[56] Unfortunately, their total number has not been transmitted in our sources and cannot be estimated even approximately, but it was in no wise comparable to that of the armed forces. The civil service included the personnel, administrative and clerical, of the central government bureaus, the agents of these bureaus throughout the provinces, and also the office staffs of the provincial governors. As a class the civil servants enjoyed a highly favored position among the inhabitants of the Empire. They were exempt from military service, enjoyed regular pay, perquisites, and promotion, and upon retirement after twenty-five years of service they received various titles, honors, and immunities. Theirs was a safe and regular career, in many respects the most peaceful and secure that one could follow in the days of the Late Empire, The only drawback was that because their rate of pay was not sufficiently high, many of them were forced to resort to making use of their official position to practice extortion upon those whom they could oppress with impunity. In fact, as time went on, the civil service became more and more a highly desired haven of refuge for those who sought to escape from the hopelessness of the hereditary careers of the *curiales, corporati,* and *coloni*. Needless to say, the government took vigorous steps to block the admission of these deserters to any of the government offices and to recover for their landlords or corporate bodies those who managed by one means or another to worm their way into an official position. Under these conditions one would not expect the government to be faced with a shortage of personnel in its civil service bureaus, unless there was a serious numerical deficiency in those elements of the population which were legally eligible for admission to these offices. And yet from the early fourth century, at least, the sons of all civil servants were bound to enter their fathers' offices, and not merely the civil service in general. This obligation is stated clearly in laws of 329 and 331, but had been created by an earlier enactment of unknown date which is referred to in the law of 329.[57] Once entered on the roll of a government office, the employee was bound to remain in it until he had completed his term of service.[58] Although these regulations applied to all bureaus in the civil administration, they were aimed in particular at the so-called *cohortales,* the employees in the lower-ranking offices, such as those of the provincial governors, who were excluded from admission to the more highly paid and honored staffs of the great palace officials. Far from suffering from a dearth of applicants for vacancies, these offices had long lists of supernumeraries eagerly awaiting to be enrolled.[59] Nevertheless, in spite of these exceptions this brief survey of the imperial civil service reveals that a shortage of available manpower was felt at least from the early fourth century and possibly from the late third. This led to the treatment of the civil servants in a manner paralleling that of soldiers serving in the armed forces.

More significant in this connection is the condition

of the third class of government servants, those who were employed in the government factories of various kinds and in other undertakings which concerned state-directed production. These were the minters (*monetarii*), the coin circulators (*collectarii* or *numularii*), the armorers (*fabricenses*), workers in the silk factories (*gynaeciarii*), weavers and garment makers in the shops which produced clothing of other materials (*linteones, linearii, linyficii, textores*), collectors of shellfish which furnished purple dye and those who made dyes therefrom (*murileguli, conchylileguli*), and workers in the government mines (*metallarii*). Along with these, I propose to consider certain employees of the government post and transport services (*bastagarii*).

The minters were the employees attached to the government mints, of which there were six in the western part of the Empire: at Rome, Aquileia, Siscia, Lugdunum, Arles, and Treves.[60] In the Early Empire the important mint at Rome had been manned by imperial slaves and freedmen, but by the time of the Late Empire the minters were all free persons, some of whom even attained the property qualification of the class of *curiales*. Those employed in each mint formed a single guild or corporation. By 317 their duties were both obligatory and hereditary, and probably they had become so at a considerably earlier date.[61] With respect to the coin circulators, it is known that in the fourth and fifth centuries in Rome they formed a corporation subject to the city prefect. At Constantinople there was a similar corporation, but they are not heard of elsewhere. Their service was obligatory and their condition hereditary.[62] The date when these regulations were imposed is not known, but it is at least reasonable to think that it corresponds to the time when duties of the minters became obligatory.

In the Late Empire the government exercised a monopoly of the manufacture of the type of clothing that was reserved for the emperor and his house. Such were silk garments dyed purple or woven with gold threads or having gold borders.[63] In addition, the government maintained factories for the production of linen clothes which were supplied to the army. Both silk works and linen factories were found in the West. Seventeen of the former and two of the latter are known to have existed.[64] For the most part, they seem to have been operated by free labor, although there were also groups of slave workers among the employees.[65] The free *gynaeciarii* and *linteones* were organized in hereditary colleges from which they were not permitted to withdraw.[66] Here again, the date at which their condition became legally fixed is unknown. As in the case of the minters, the properties of the free garment workers had to be used for the maintenance of their trade and could not be transferred from the service of the corporation to which they belonged.[67] Once more the government policy indicates a dearth of skilled craftsmen available for what were regarded as essential occupations.

Not only the manufacture of purple garments, but even the procurement and processing of the necessary dyes became government monopolies in the Late Empire, probably in the time of Diocletian.[68] Hence, the government took into its service the fishermen who gathered the shellfish from which the dyes were extracted, as well as all others engaged in the purple dye industry.[69] The *murileguli* formed a number of guilds in the West as well as in the East. They were free persons, but their membership in the corporations was both obligatory and hereditary from at least the early fourth century. Their properties were liable to confiscation if they failed to produce their assigned quota of shellfish. Additional proof of a dearth of numbers in this occupation is furnished by several laws of the Theodosian Code. In 371 the emperors Valentian, Valens, and Gratian declared that any outsider taking a wife who was attached to a guild of *conchylileguli* must himself become bound to her status.[70] In 424 *murileguli* who had managed to obtain forbidden government positions were recalled to their original condition, and in 425 the sons of daughters of these dye collectors, no matter who their fathers were, had to accept the status of their mothers, which was a logical inference from the constitution of 371.[71] Only under special circumstances might a dye worker, a minter, or an imperial weaver be freed from his guild and its obligations; even then he must leave a competent substitute, and both his property and his descendants remained subject to his previous service.[72] The repeated attempts of private persons to entice imperial weavers into their own employment also argue for a shortage of skilled craftsmen in this trade.[73]

Another important government industry was the manufacture of armor and weapons of war. This was also a state monopoly.[74] The work was carried on in government arsenals of which there were twenty in the western provinces.[75] These arsenals were manned by free members, the *fabricenses*. Like other government employees of this sort they formed a guild or corporation at each manufacturing establishment and were placed under a hereditary obligation.[76] There are some other indications that a considerable shortage of armorers existed. Late in the fourth century they were branded on the arm so that they could readily be identified if they deserted their arsenals and could be dragged back to them.[77] Public slaves also had to be assigned to work in the arsenals. If any of them married a slave woman belonging to an armorer, he, along with his wife and children, was assigned to the factory of his wife's owner.[78]

Under Roman law mineral deposits belonged to the state, and their exploitation always remained under government control. The same was true of certain stone quarries. During the Republic and in the early Principate the mines were worked by contractors who leased the right to do so from the state. But gradually they all came to be operated directly by the government. This remained the rule in the Late Empire, although there were some exceptions.[79] The production of marble had fallen off to such an extent that the administration was seriously concerned about both its scarcity and its high price. Accordingly, all private owners of marble quarries were encouraged to put them in operation and to keep them in production. When they failed to do so, permission was given to anyone who pleased to work these private quarries upon payment of one-tenth of the income therefrom to the owner and another tenth to the state.[80] This situation clearly shows that there was a great dearth of quarrymen, for otherwise the high price of marble would have made its marketing a very profitable enterprise. The government itself undertook the operation of all imperial quarries as well as all mines. The operatives were for the most part free persons, organized in local corporations.[81] They were not allowed to desert the mines or quarries in which they labored, and their occupations and obligations were inherited by their children.[82] Their numbers, which were always inadequate, were reinforced by convicted persons condemned to the mines.[83] There was a particularly acute shortage of gold miners (*aurileguli*) to whom in 365 the emperors Valentinian and Valens offered special inducements to find new deposits of ore and to work them.[84] But both they and the other miners and quarrymen were too few to meet the heavy demands made upon them by the state. Until the collapse of the Western Empire in the fifth century the government engaged in a constant struggle to prevent their escape to distant areas and other occupations.[85]

Since the government of the Late Empire received many of its tax payments in kind as well as in money and was also actively engaged in various productive enterprises, it was obliged to maintain an elaborate organization for the transport of government goods, quite apart from that which served to supply the needs of the city of Rome. One important group of transport workers were the *bastagarii,* who seem to have been the owners of, or at least had the obligation to furnish, baggage animals.[86] Like the other groups of government agents discussed, the *bastagarii* were enrolled in hereditary corporations. As in the case of the others, the government had to intervene to prevent them from deserting their corporations for some other occupation.[87] Here, too, it is justifiable to interpret these measures of government control as indicative of a shortage of numbers.

It has been seen, then, that the condition of the employees in the various manufacturing, mining, and transportation operations carried on by the government of the Late Empire reveals a manpower shortage similar to that which existed among the *curiales,* the municipal corporations, and the colleges assigned to the service of providing supplies of food for the city of Rome. Their capital of all kinds is attached by the state to the conduct of their particular occupation and cannot be used in any other activity, their persons become bound to virtually lifelong service in the same occupation, and their children inherit the status and obligations of their parents.

From the foregoing survey of the government services of the Late Roman Empire, particularly in the West, the following conclusions may be drawn. The military establishment suffered from a constant and ever-increasing shortage of manpower, a shortage which contributed materially to its decline in numbers and in efficiency. Even the civil service, whose members enjoyed a peculiarly favorable status among the population in general, suffered somewhat from the same trouble, although here the shortage of personnel was felt only in the provincial and not in the central government offices. And the hereditary corporations of government workers in industry, mining, and transportation experienced an initial manpower deficit which became ever more and more serious throughout the fourth and fifth centuries.

V

Manpower Shortage and the Fall of Rome

IN THIS LAST CHAPTER of the book I shall try to sum up the conclusions at which I arrived in the foregoing chapters and also to correlate manpower shortage with the other major factors that contributed to the collapse of the West Roman Empire in the fifth century. Let me make it clear at this point that I do not believe there was any single major cause of this collapse, but rather a combination of conditions, forces, and trends which interacted upon one another so that at times it is almost impossible to tell which was cause and which was effect. Nor do I believe it possible to indicate with any degree of exactness the point at which recessions began. Furthermore, I do not believe there was uniformity of conditions through the Western Empire as a whole, and I am quite prepared to admit that the process of decay may for a time have been arrested and, within limited areas, even temporarily reversed.

It is my conviction that I have been able to present convincing reasons, partly on the basis of contemporary evidence and partly on the strength of deductions drawn from the demographic history of other peoples, for believing that a shortage in manpower had developed within the Roman Empire as early as the last quarter of the second century. In my opinion this shortage of manpower is to be associated with, and was caused by, an actual retrogression of certain elements of the population, in particular the inhabitants of the rural areas. In this I see the explanation of such a phenomenon as the inability of the Emperor Marcus Aurelius to find the needed recruits for his army among the Romans and provincials and his resort to the importation of barbarians to make up the deficit. By the beginning of the third century manpower shortage was felt to be affecting the population of the towns also. Here, as an important factor may be seen the legacy of the great plague of the years 166 to 180. At any rate, Septimius Severus and others of his dynasty admitted the situation and sought to combat by legislative means some of its consequences. Their attempts to encourage agriculture and increase the rural population, their closer supervision of the occupational groups whose services appeared essential to the conduct of public business, and their impressment of the town councils as tax collecting agencies reflect both a shortage in production and a scarcity of manpower.[1]

It has been demonstrated that by 235 the Roman Empire was showing definite symptoms of impoverishment in its human and in its material resources. I do not believe that this can be accounted for to any major extent by the effects of the war between Septimius Severus and Clodius Albinus with its resultant confiscation of the estates of the leading supporters of Severus' defeated rival. Only the proprietors and not the tillers of the soil would be affected by the change of ownership of rural estates, and the land itself would not be withdrawn from production. It is quite impossible to gauge the effects of Severus' policy upon persons engaged in commerce and industry. But the impoverishment of the urban middle class, which begins to become apparent on a wide scale in the early third century, can best be explained as a result of the impoverishment and decline of the surrounding rural population.[2] The latter furnished the manpower to till the estates of the urban proprietors, they were the consumers of the products of local manufacture, and they were also the natural source of immigrants needed to counterbalance the normal decline in urban birth rate.

A good many years ago, in addressing a meeting of the Michigan Academy of Science, Arts, and Letters, I took occasion to emphasize the part which taxation played in the economic breakdown of the Roman Empire.[3] I pointed out that by the third century the burden of taxation had become so heavy that it had begun to consume the capital resources of the taxpayers. This was due to the increasing costs of the imperial administration without any corresponding increase in production on the part of the population of the Empire. For this failure more than one factor was responsible. Among the causes may be mentioned the great dependence of industry upon slave labor, the lack of inventions which would stimulate production, the absence of copyright, and the unfavorable status of investors in business enterprises under Romany law. Agriculture was the main source of wealth, and production in agriculture depended upon manpower. An increase in the rural population, therefore, would have resulted in greater production, but a stationary or decreasing agrarian element would have caused stagnation or actual decline in agricultural products. As I have tried to show, there was a positive shortage of rural labor by the third century. Consequently, the increases in taxation coincided with a falling off in production and in manpower. The result was bound to be a heavier weight of taxation for the survivors and their gradual impoverishment, which, in turn, would cause a decrease in the public revenues.

It would, of course, be utterly impossible to calculate the total population loss between the death of Marcus Aurelius in 180 and that of Severus Alexander in 235. It would be just as much out of the question to try to estimate the decline in the birth rate. There were almost certainly areas where such symptoms had not yet become apparent, for example, in sections of North Africa, where the municipalities continued to expand until later in the third century. But these favorable conditions were due to special circumstances and cannot be made the basis for generalizations about Italy and the western provinces as a whole.

It has been seen how the disorders of the troubled period 235 to 284 were bound to have an extremely unfavorable effect upon the population, both rural and urban. Not only must the actual loss of life have been extremely heavy and the average longevity correspondingly reduced, but the rate of decline must have been greatly accelerated. To judge from later parallels, the population of the Roman world can hardly have recovered from the delayed effects of the epidemic of the time of Marcus Aurelius before it was struck by the equally severe and even longer pestilence of the middle third century.[4] Also, the added losses due to war, starvation, and forcible deportation must be taken into account. Once the birth rate of a people starts to decline, it continues to do so in a geometrical and not merely an arithmetical ratio.[5] The conclusion must therefore be reached that if even a slight decline were evident by 235, as a result of total population loss, the rate would be very noticeable by 284. Furthermore, it would keep on becoming increasingly rapid unless or until a countertrend were established.

On the analogy of the experience of other countries, it would take a very long time even under favorable conditions for this countertrend to become effective. It is only too well known that such favorable conditions never came into being during the fourth and fifth centuries. And the evidence I have presented from the period 284–476 indicates that, in spite of the restoration of a large measure of internal peace, and notwithstanding the voluntary and involuntary immigration of barbarian peoples, the population trend was steadily downward until the end of the West Roman Empire. Herein lies the explanation of the continued decline in the population of western Europe until about 900, a phenomenon noted by students of medieval demography.

The inevitable accompaniment of the population

decline was naturally a corresponding decrease in the manpower available for agriculture, industry, and the public services, a condition which became more and more acute from the late third to the fifth century. At the same time there was a corresponding decrease in agricultural and industrial production. It would be rash to say that this was due altogether to shortage of available labor since the economic policies of the Late Empire unquestionably played a considerable role in preventing a revival of prosperity. The decline in individual capital wealth was also a factor of importance. In general, both in agriculture and in industry, there was a very definite correlation between the number of workers available and the quantity of production. Insufficiency of agricultural production in its turn reacted upon the ability of the population to maintain itself. Taken together, all of these factors produced an overall condition of impoverishment which offers the fundamental explanation of the social and economic policy of the government of the Late Empire.

Undoubtedly, the ultimate objective of Diocletian and his successors was the preservation of the Empire. And it is equally beyond question that, with the exception of some weaklings in the West during the fifth century, the rulers of the Late Empire devoted themselves conscientiously and unsparingly to this task. It seems equally clear that for them the cardinal problems were the maintenance of internal order and the defense of the frontiers. Each of these problems required the presence of a strong, loyal, and efficient army. Since the peculiar geographical situation of the Roman Empire, strung out as it was around the shores of the Mediterranean Sea, gave it frontiers whose length was out of proportion to its superficial area, and since the internal lines of communication were correspondingly extended as well as interrupted by the Mediterranean and its tributary waters, the size of the standing army had to be considerably larger than would have been required in a more compact state.[6] Furthermore, the frontiers were under continuous attack or threat of attack from Persians and barbarians, so that, far from reducing the military establishment, Diocletian felt that he must actually increase it. The emperors of the fourth century tried to maintain the army at the level set by him, or even to strengthen somewhat its effectives. There could be no question of their reviving the citizen militia armies of the days of the Republic. They had to accept the professional, long-service army developed under the Early Empire, although they might and did modify its internal organization.

As has been seen, in trying to enlarge and maintain such an army the emperors were faced with a shortage of suitable recruits, caused in large measure by the decline of the rural population. Hence they found themselves on the horns of a dilemma. Either they could conscript Roman civilians for military service and so decrease still further production and the state revenues, or they could adopt and employ on a larger scale the policy initiated by Marcus Aurelius, followed by other emperors, and resorted to much more widely by Probus, namely, to make up the deficit with barbarians. It would be naïve to think that the imperial government was blind to the dangers of such a policy.

That they adopted it, is a clear indication of the acute problem of available manpower within the empire. It led, inevitably, to the gradual barbarization of the army, that is, to the predominance of the barbarian element both in the ranks and in the officer corps, even including the commanding generals. It led also to the wholesale settlement of barbarian colonies within the western provinces as feeders for the army. These groups were not assimilated into the Roman citizen body. A vigorous and expanding population could have absorbed them, but not the enfeebled and discouraged one of the Late Empire. Yet in spite of these settlements, shortage of manpower for the army continued and this, coupled with decreasing revenues, led the state to resort to the subsidization of actually autonomous, although nominally dependent, barbarian tribes as federate allies under the obligation to defend the frontiers. The inability of the Roman government to prevent the settlement of these allies as well as other invaders within the Empire, coupled with the passing of the command of the army of the West into the hands of barbarian king makers was the immediate cause of the disintegration of the Western Empire.

I should be the last person to claim that the fall of the West Roman Empire can be explained solely in terms of a problem of shortage of recruits for the army. In an article published a few years ago I tried to evaluate the role of policy or, to put it otherwise, of the lack of astute statesmanship in bringing about this catastrophe.[7] There I called attention to the way in which the eastern emperors prevented their military organization from being dominated by a barbarian element and reduced the menace of barbarian invasions, whereas their western colleagues were unsuccessful in trying to shake off these perils. One of the main reasons why the eastern emperors were able to accomplish this was that they found a source of recruits in the Romanized population of the East with which to counterbalance their Germanic mercenaries. That West Rome failed to do so adds still further testimony to the lack of manpower at its disposal.

It has been held by some historians that it was not scarcity of recruits but lack of military spirit among the Romans that caused the emperors to depend to such a great extent upon barbarians.[8] No doubt, under the system of recruitment which was practiced there was a tendency for the landholder to supply recruits of inferior physique who lacked the necessary military qualities. No doubt also, there was a great deal of self-mutilation to avoid military service, and desertions were only too frequent.[9] The reason why such a poor type of recruit was furnished by the Roman element is to be found in the lack of suitable men who could be spared from essential production, as well as in the indifference of the *coloni* and other hereditary working groups toward the fate of a government which seemed to them more brutal in its exactions than did the barbarians. The Gauls, however, made excellent soldiers and so did the Illyrians, only there were not enough of them. Vegetius, in discussing the deficiency of suitable recruits, gives priority to decline of population over aversion to military life caused by urbanization.[10]

Not only did the emperors require a large standing army to support their authority within the Empire and to defend it against attack from without, but they also had to maintain a system of civil government adequate for the administration of justice and, above all, for the collection of the taxes requisite for defraying the military and civil expenditures of the state. Here, again, they were the heirs of a long tradition which had resulted in the growth of a highly centralized bureaucracy. It would have been futile to think of replacing this with some decentralized system that might have been less expensive but, from the point of view of the emperors, less efficient and less subject to supervision and control. As it was, the attempt to enforce the economic and social reforms and to extract as large a revenue as possible from the civilian population led to increased departmentalization of the bureaucracy and also to an increase in the number of the civil service employees. This coincided with the replacement of imperial slaves and freedmen in the office staffs by salaried persons of free birth, a policy which had begun under the Early Empire and had been hastened by the decrease in the number of slaves available. As I have pointed out, the extent to which this produced a drain upon the civilian population cannot be estimated, but it did, undoubtedly, add to the number of nonproducers and correspondingly increased the cost of government. This in turn made the burden of the taxpayers still heavier and, under the declining economic conditions, led to further impoverishment.

If these essential military and civil services were to be maintained, the necessary government revenues had to be assured. Consequently, the emperors must find a way of raising adequate taxes when production was

falling off and the manpower required for production
was decreasing. Diocletian, who initiated the economic
policy followed and elaborated by his successors, attempted a twofold solution. He introduced a complete
revision of the tax system which was intended to place
at the disposal of the treasury a constant flow of agricultural produce through regular taxation instead of
resorting to irregular levies, and, as a necessary corol-
lary, he bound agricultural workers to the soil in order
to prevent a decline in production. This step can be
explained only in the light of a shortage of agricultural labor and the fear that this shortage would grow
more acute through the flight of farm tenants and
workers. In all probability the decision to collect all
taxes on land in natural produce and to pay soldiers
and other government employees in allowances instead
of in money was made in part because of the shortage
of silver money and the virtual worthlessness of the
coinage then in circulation. But there was also another
important reason, namely, the shortage in agricultural
production which, combined with the depreciation of
the coinage, had led to high prices and a general increase in the cost of living. As has recently been pointed
out, the payment of salaries in kind protected the recipients against a rise in prices and also, when they had
surplus allowances, permitted them to make a profit
by selling on the open market. It is a mistake to think
that there was any general abandonment of a money
economy and a return to a so-called natural one.[11] In
this connection it should be recalled that Diocletian
began, and Constantine I completed, the stabilization
of the gold and silver coinage, and also that during

the later fourth and fifth centuries the government was able to pay a certain number of its employees in coin instead of in allowances if they so preferred. Furthermore, taxes other than those imposed on farm land continued to be paid in money. The eastern half of the Empire, as is known, had large quantities of gold at its disposal, particularly in the fifth and subsequent centuries. Thus, it would be rash to conclude that currency shortage was a major factor in the collapse of the Empire in the West. Shortage of production was more significant.

At this point, it might be worth while to consider briefly the view that the decrease in agricultural production was due to a condition of soil exhaustion which affected the Empire as a whole. I am in agreement with those who reject this theory.[12] Beyond all question Greece, the Italian peninsula, and Sicily had suffered greatly from soil erosion and consequent soil impoverishment, which was an important factor in the decline of agriculture and of the rural population in these areas. But no such condition has been demonstrated for the Po Valley, the Rhine and Danubian lands, Gaul, Britain, and North Africa, or even for Spain, although it is possible that it had begun to affect parts of that peninsula. In the light of present knowledge of soil conditions in the Late Empire, the shortage of agricultural products must be attributed largely to shortage of rural labor and a failure to develop improved methods of cultivation and improved farm machinery which might have compensated for the decrease in manpower.

The collection of the land taxes in kind had important consequences for the commercial and industrial classes of the Empire. Of itself, the handling of income in natural products did not create any new problem for the government. From the beginning of recorded history the governments of Mediterranean and Near Eastern states had been used to raising and disbursing revenues of this sort. They were thoroughly familiar with all problems of transportation, warehousing, and distribution. And Rome was no exception. One need only recall that the land taxes of more than one province had been collected in kind, that from the later days of the Republic the government had imported a large part of the grain consumed in the capital, and that the Romans had had abundant experience in collecting and transporting army stores on a large scale. Consequently, the increase in revenues in kind merely required an increase in the number of granaries and other storehouses, of ships, of wagons and pack animals, and of persons engaged in handling and transporting government stores. Since, however, a very large amount of the wheat, barley, wine, oil, and other agricultural products contributed as taxes would be consumed by the soldiers and civil servants stationed in the areas where they were collected, this increase in facilities need not have been very extensive. Under the Republic and Early Empire the movement of government goods had been effected by contracts with private individuals or groups of individuals and in the third century by contracts with special guilds, in so far as this was not taken care of by the widespread system of *munera* or obligatory services imposed on the municipalities of the provinces. In most modern states an expansion of governmental activities of a comparable sort would have been taken care of by private agencies competing voluntarily for the opportunity to secure government contracts. This would have occurred also at an earlier time in Roman history. But at the close of the third century there were not enough contractors with the capital needed for undertaking such contracts and not enough manpower available for carrying them out if they had been undertaken by companies or by individual businessmen.

Faced by this shortage of contractors and workers, the government resorted to conscription. By developing to the utmost the principle of public obligations incumbent on both persons and property, they bound to the public service the capital and the persons deemed essential in the collecting of levies of all kinds and the proper handling of the various sorts of government supplies. Thus, the municipal councilors, the corporations of shipowners and transport workers, as well as the similar corporations of merchants and others engaged in processing or selling grain, wine, oil, and various sorts of meat for Rome (and later for Constantinople), found themselves reduced to the status of involuntary government employees. As members of these guilds or corporations they were compelled to serve the state either without, or at best with inadequate, compensation.

The same basic factor, the shortage of manpower for public service, brought about the impressment of the members of the municipal corporations throughout the Empire and of their capital into public service. The immediate reasons might vary from one type of cor-

poration to another, but in every instance the under-
lying cause was an actual or a feared shortage of personnel for services which the imperial government
deemed necessary for the proper maintenance of municipal life or for the proper performance of the part
which the municipalities had to play in the whole system
of local, provincial, and imperial administration. This
obligation was extended even to the actors' guilds,
whose members were bound just as strictly as were the
carpenters, masons, and rug makers, who acted as the
municipal fire brigades. The only distinction between
the condition of these local guilds and that of those who
served the needs of urban Rome was that their services
were not so continuously in demand. Most of their
munera, however, had to be performed without compensation. In addition, all persons engaged in trade and
industry were subjected to an onerous tax collected in
gold and silver money.

Another result of the shortage and uncertainties of
production was the taking over by the state of the manufacturing of arms and armor and, to a larger extent,
clothing for the army. This additional encroachment
upon the field of private enterprise may have been
somewhat motivated by a desire to maintain a government monopoly of weapons of warfare as a means of
controlling brigandage and insurrection.[13] But coming
as it did upon the heels of the economic collapse in the
third century, it finds its chief explanation in the inability of private manufacturers to supply government
needs in this area of production. On the other hand, the
state monopoly of the production of certain types of
silk goods and of purple dyes was not so much the re-

sult of any shortage of production as of the desire to reserve for members of the imperial court and high government officials the use of silk garments and also of the purple dye which had come to be associated with autocracy. This was all in accordance with the policy of emphasizing the sacredness of the imperial household and the great gulf that separated the emperor from the rest of the population. Since the supply of silk in the Mediterranean area before the importation of the silkworm from China in the middle of the sixth century was very limited, the monopoly of the production of silk goods was easy to establish and maintain. Like the monopoly of the manufacture of red dyes from certain species of shellfish which seem to have become scarce, that of silk manufacture had little effect upon the economy of the Empire in the West. As has been seen, however, in operating these enterprises as well as the government arsenals and clothing establishments, the state encountered difficulties arising from a shortage of labor. In its desperate attempt to maintain production it felt compelled to resort to the imposing of a permanent hereditary obligation upon its employees.

Having traced the part of manpower shortage in determining the military and economic policy of the Late Roman Empire, I shall now consider the effects of this policy upon the population situation. Did it create conditions under which population, and with it production, could increase and prosperity be restored? The answer is emphatically in the negative. The restoration of more peaceful internal conditions by the early fourth century did unquestionably lead to a temporary improvement in agriculture in some areas and to the rise of some new urban centers. And this improvement would naturally operate as a brake upon the rate of population decrease. But, unfortunately, it was neither general nor sustained. The crushing load of taxation and obligatory government services proved too great for the producing classes to support. They did not have the wherewithal to raise and support families large enough to maintain, much less increase, their numbers from one generation to the next. Their lives were so burdensome that each of the obligatory occupation groups sought to escape from its status. The army, the civil service, and the clergy seemed havens of refuge for many. Farm workers tried to enter one of the town corporations or deserted their fields to swell the numbers of brigands or to join troups of invading barbarians. Town councilors even sought to hide themselves as hereditary tenants on the estates of the great landholders. People of various classes took to the forests or the desert to avoid the eyes of government officials. The result was a still further decrease in the manpower available for private or public production. Under such circumstances the government reacted as might have been expected. It tried to tighten the system of controls by which it regulated the lives of the vast majority of the population. Law after law reiterated the life-long obligation of the individual to his particular class or corporation and its activities, the perpetual lien of the state, municipality, or college upon his property for financing the performance of its functions, the hereditability of his status by his heirs, the ban upon attempts to alter one's inherited condition, and the prohibition to change one's place of residence. But all to no purpose. Conditions grew stead-

ily worse. By the early fifth century the area of untilled land had reached astonishing proportions, and
many of the cities had become ghost towns.

But someone may raise the question, how is such a
state of affairs compatible with the building activities
of the emperors of the time, with the multitude of
churches that arose in the fourth and fifth centuries in
Italy and the western provinces, or with the opulence
of the homes of the upper classes and the apparently
easy circumstances in which they lived? How can it be
reconciled with the maintenance of the free distribution
of food for the city proletariat of Rome at the expense
of the government? The explanation is not difficult.
In so far as the emperors were concerned, they were
caught in the toils of tradition and felt that as far as
possible they must live up to the standards set by their
predecessors. A display of public munificence had to be
maintained if an emperor were not to lose prestige in
the eyes of his subjects. And loss of prestige might
foster discontent and lead to the support of a rival. It
probably never even occurred to one of the late emperors to abandon the distribution of free bread, oil,
and wine to the Roman mob, however much that might
have reduced government expenses and however many
persons and however much private capital it might have
released for profitable enterprises. No better proof is
required of the influence of tradition in this respect than
Constantine's granting of similar donations to the
residents of his new capital, Constantinople. But, as a
matter of fact, after the age of Diocletian and Constantine I, few great buildings were erected in the western part of the Empire, and even for the adornment of

Constantine's own arch in Rome an earlier monument
had to be despoiled. A large number of the churches of
the time were remodeled pagan temples or were built
from the ruins of public buildings no longer requisite
for the decreasing population of Rome and other cities,
nor did they compare in size or elegance with the great
structures of earlier days. The wealthy aristocracy of
the Late Empire was composed of inner circles of the
senatorial order. They were the great landholders who
furnished the higher officials of the bureaucracy and, to
some extent, of the army. Their estates grew as the
smaller proprietors were sold out by the government or
handed over their properties to their more influential
neighbors and became their serfs rather than face the
imperial tax collectors. They, too, acquired abandoned
lands which the government offered to any who could
afford to till them, and who but the very wealthy could
do so? The majority of them no longer lived in the
cities but in large country villas, at times fortified, sur-
rounded by their dependent serfs. There, relying upon
their influence in the administration and even at times
resorting to armed force, they could mitigate or defy
the demands of government agents. These few grew
relatively richer, as the middle classes were reduced to
beggary and almost disappeared, and the poorer sank
to even lower levels of wretchedness.

It might possibly be asked, Why did not the extensive
settlement of Germanic people within the Empire reverse the downward population trend in the rural
areas? Possibly it did in some districts and during brief
periods, for the Romans in earlier times considered
that the families of these barbarians were larger than

theirs. In many places the new settlers were numerous enough to have the memory of their presence perpetuated in the names of rural communities.[14] But there is no proof of any permanent beneficial effects, and even after the settlement of the larger tribes of barbarian conquerors, the downward trend continued. For this the following observations may offer at least a partial explanation. The Germans, like the other peoples of ancient times, had a high rate of infant mortality and a low average longevity, both of which kept down the rate of population increase. Furthermore, the lot of those who were settled as *coloni* on the properties of rural proprietors was little removed from slavery. Like the rest of the peasants attached to the soil, they came to feel the double pressure of the demands of their landlords and of the state, and their share of their crops was reduced to the bare subsistence level. This gave no encouragement to the raising of any large families, but it did encourage desertion of the lands to which they were in bondage. A life of brigandage or the opportunity of joining a band of barbarian marauders would seem infinitely preferable to the thankless toil to which they had been condemned. On the other hand, those who were settled in groups on state land with the obligation to furnish recruits to the Roman army found their young men taken in large numbers into service. Although these were permitted to marry, their life was not conducive to the raising of a numerous progeny and their average longevity doubtless fell well below that of those not engaged in military service. At any rate, the ever-increasing shortage of recruits indicates that they were not very prolific since, as will be remembered, the sons of soldiers and veterans came to be obligated to follow the paternal profession. In this connection it may be worth while to repeat that for some centuries after the settlement of the larger barbarian tribes— Visigoths, Burgundians, Franks, and so forth—within the formers limits of the western Empire, no rise in population appears to have taken place.

Did the expansion of Christianity, with its higher standards of morality and greater stress on family life have any influence upon the downward trend of population? The answer is that its effects must have been very slight. Christianity was at first an urban religion, and its spread among the rural population in the fourth and fifth centuries was relatively slow. So it came about that the term *paganus,* "countryman," was used to describe a non-Christian, a "pagan." The urban population, as has been seen, kept on declining along with the rural. It is true that during these centuries the West did not experience the rush of Christian men and women to monasteries and convents that characterized the East. But all the same, the favorable attitude of the Christians towards celibacy was just as notable in the West as elsewhere. And at this time the Christians did not in general favor large families, as is shown by Eusebius' explanation of the Christian attitude on the question.[15]

And so, with declining manpower and increasing impoverishment, the Roman Empire in the West, unable to defend itself against disintegration from within and invasion from without, staggered slowly on to its inevitable dissolution.

Notes

I

[1] A. H. M. Jones, *Ancient Economic History* (London: H. K. Lewis, 1948), pp. 14-17.

[2] *History of the Later Roman Empire* . . . (London and New York, 1889), I, 25. See also J. W. Thompson, *An Economic and Social History of the Middle Ages 300-1300* (New York and London: Century Co., [1928]), pp. 50-62.

[3] A. Dopsch, *The Economic and Social Foundations of European Civilization*. Eng. trans. (London: K. Paul, Trench, Trubner, and Co., 1937), p. 53.

[4] *L'Empire romain. Evolution et décadence* (Paris: E. Flammarion, 1922), p. 252.

[5] *L'Empire chrétien (325-395)*, Vol. IV, Pt. 2, of *Histoire générale: Histoire romaine*, ed. by G. Glotz (Paris: Presses Univ. de France, 1947), p. 412.

[6] Julius Beloch, *Die Bevölkerung der griechisch-römischen Welt* (Leipzig, 1886), pp. 7-12. The same point has been made very forcefully by A. H. M. Jones, *op. cit.*, pp. 1-10. See also A. Momigliano, "Popolazione," in the *Enciclopedia italiana*, XXVII, 914; Beloch, "Die Bevölkerung Europas im Mittelalter," *Zeitschr. f. Socialwiss.*, 3 (1900), 405.

[7] See E. Ciccotti, *Indirizzi e metodi degli studi di demografia antica*, Prefazione of *Bibliotheca di storia economica*, ed. V. Pareto (Milan, 1909), IV, vii-ciii. He goes so far as to deny the possibility of making any reliable calculation of the population of the Greco-Roman world.

[8] *Bevölkerung der griechisch-römischen Welt*, p. 502.

[9] *The End of the Ancient World* . . . , tr. by P. and M. Leon (New York: A. A. Knopf, 1931), pp. 65-67.

[10] *Geschichte des spätrömischen Reiches* (Vienna: L. W. Seidel und Sohn, 1928), I, 3.

[11] H. Delbrück, *Geschichte der Kriegskunst* (Berlin: G. Stilke, 1921), II, 237-38; so also Beloch, "Die Bevölkerung im Altertum," *Zeitschr. f. Socialwiss.*, 2 (1899), 619.

[12] Stein, *op. cit.*, I, 3.

[13] *The Invasions of Europe by the Barbarians* (London: Macmillan and Co., 1928), p. 38.

[14] Piganiol, *op. cit.*, p. 413.

[15] *Bevölkerung der griechisch-römischen Welt*, p. 411.

[16] "Frumentatio" in De Ruggiero, *Dizionario epigrafico,* III (1922), 308-11. Cardinali gives a résumé of earlier estimates. A later one is found in G. Gigli, *La Crisi dell'impero romano* (Palermo: G. B. Palumbo, 1947), pp. 161-66. Cf. T. Frank (ed.), *Economic Survey of Ancient Rome* (Baltimore: Johns Hopkins Press, 1940), V, 218, and Beloch, *op. cit.*, p. 405, n. 1ª.

[17] Kahrstedt in L. Friedlaender, *Darstellungen aus der Sittengeschichte Roms . . .* , eds. 9-10 (Leipzig: S. Hirzel, 1921), IV, 11-12.

[18] A. von Gerkan, "Die Einwohnerzahl Roms in der Kaiserzeit," *Römische Mittheilungen,* 55 (1940), 149 ff.

[19] G. Calza and G. Lugli, "La Popolazione di Roma antica," *Bull. communale,* 69 (1941), 24.

[20] Lot, *op. cit.*, p. 70. He gives 200,000-250,000 for the time of Constantine. Lot's figures are supported by R. Latouche, "Aspect demographique de la crise des grandes invasions," *Population,* 1947, pp. 681-90.

[21] Cf. Bloch, *op. cit.*, p. 252, who points out that specific statements by ancient writers at times make up for the lack of statistics.

[22] W. F. Willcox, "The Length of Life in the Roman Empire. A Methodological Note," *Congrès international de la population* (Paris, 1937), II *(Demographie historique),* 22.

[23] Karl Pearson, "On the Change in Expectation of Life in Man During a Period of Circa 2000 Years," *Biometrika,* I (1901-2), 261-64. Cf. "Longevity from Ancient to Modern Times," *Metropolitan Life Insurance Co. Statistical Bull.,* Oct., 1947, pp. 1-3.

[24] Willcox, *op. cit.*, pp. 21-22. In this article the author shows that on methodological grounds many of the conclusions of the following studies must be rejected: Karl Pearson, *op. cit.;* Atilio di Marchi, "Cifre di mortalità nelle inscrizione romane," *Real. Inst. Lombardo di Scienze e Lettere,* ser. II, 336 (1930), 1025-34; and W. R. Macdonell, "On the Expectation of Life in Ancient Rome and in the Provinces of Hispania, Lusitania and Africa,"

Biometrika, 9 (1913-14), 366-80, but at the same time he shows that the data collected by Macdonell in particular point to the low life expectancy that has been cited. On the basis of further evidence the whole problem has been restudied with great care by A. R. Burn, "Hic breve vivitur. A Study of the Expectation of Life in the Roman Empire," *Past and Present,* 4 (1953), 1-31. In general, Burn approves Willcox's strictures on the work of di Marchi and Macdonell, but points out that he is mistaken in challenging the conclusion that women had a shorter life expectancy than men in the Roman world. The impressive set of life tables which Burn has appended to his article demonstrates beyond question that the death rate in the Roman Empire was by modern standards exceedingly high and that consequently the contemporary life expectancy corresponded to that of the countries with the lowest known life expectancy in recent times. I am indebted to the kindness of Professor Willcox for a reprint of Mr. Burn's article.

[25] M. Hombert and C. Preaux, "Note sur la durée de la vie dans l'Egypt greco-romaine," *Chronique d'Egypt,* 39-40 (1945), 139-46, and "A propos des chances de survie dans l'Empire romain," *Latomus,* v (1946), 91-97. From a study of 813 cases the authors find that the average age at death was 32.39 years, which gives a corrected birth expectancy of 23.78 years. Their figure of 32.39 years has received striking confirmation from a study of 121 funerary stelae from Terenouthis, now in the University of Michigan Kelsey Museum of Archaeology, made by Dr. Finley A. Hooper, who found that the average recorded age of the deceased was 32.87 years. On the life expectancy at birth in Roman Egypt, see also Pearson, *op. cit.,* who arrives at an estimate of 31 for well-to-do persons; and A. Landry, "Quelques aperçus concernant la dépopulation dans l'antiquité greco-romaine," *Rev. hist.,* 77 (1936), 26, n. 3, who deduces a life expectancy of not much over twenty years from the data collected by A. Calderini, *La Composizione della famiglia secondo le schede di censimento dell' Egitto romano* (Milan: Soc. editrice "Vita e pensiero," [1923?]), p. 47.

[26] Burn, *op. cit.,* p. 21. The figures for India in 1946 were 26.91 years for men and 26.56 for women, *Population Index,* 1946, pp. 243-44. For China in the years 1940-44 they were 33.8 years for men and 38 years for women not counting the deaths from

cholera which reduced these to 31.9 and 34, respectively, *op. cit.,* 1947, p. 94.

[27] Willcox, *op. cit.* p. 21. In 1946 the life expectancy for men in Italy was 53.76 years, for women 56 years; in France 54.30 and 59.02; for the United Kingdom 60.18 and 64.40; for the United States 63.16 and 68.27 (*Pop. Ind.,* 1946, pp. 243-44). In 1948 the comparable figures for Greece were 49.09 and 50.89; for Portugal 48.58 and 52.82; and for Egypt only 30.02 and 31.5 (*op. cit.,* 1948, p. 279).

[28] Notably by J. C. Russell in "Late Medieval Population Patterns," *Speculum,* XX (1945), 160, and in his *British Medieval Population* (Albuquerque: Univ. New Mexico Press, 1948), pp. 180-88. The English life expectancy at birth prior to 1276 was about 35 years. From 1276 to 1450 it fluctuated chiefly owing to the Black Death from 17.33 to 32.75 years. See also Russell's "Length of Life in England, 1250-1348," *Human Biology,* 9 (1937), 528-41.

[29] The following data are taken from the article of Russell just cited, pp. 157-71.

[30] On this point see Lynn White, Jr., "Technology and Economics in the Middle Ages," *Speculum,* XV (1940), 141-55.

[31] Willcox, *op. cit.,* p. 21, and note 27, above.

[32] The summary given in the text is based on Ta Chen, "Population in Modern China," *Amer. Journ. Sociol.,* LII (1946), Pt. 2.

[33] A. Landry, *op. cit.,* p. 23. On the failure of city people to replace themselves with children, the differential birth rate between city and country, and urbanization as a major factor in producing a falling birth rate not only in towns but also in rural areas, see W. S. Thompson, *Population Problems* (New York and London: McGraw-Hill Book Co., 1930), pp. 122-26, and *Plenty of People* (New York: Ronald Press), 1948, pp. 147-50; T. Lynn Smith, *Population Analysis* (New York: McGraw-Hill Book Co., 1948), pp. 230-32.

[34] Russell, *op. cit.,* p. 164.

[35] See Landry, *op. cit.,* p. 23.

[36] Ta Chen, *op. cit.,* 3. On fluctuations in population among ancient peoples, see J. L. Myres, "The Causes of Rise and Fall in the Population of the Ancient World," *Eugenics Review,* VII (1915-16), 15-45, who emphasizes economic and social factors.

[37] A. C. Johnson, *Roman Egypt*, in *An Economic Survey of Ancient Rome*, ed. by T. Frank (Baltimore: Johns Hopkins Press, 1936), II, 245-46; Seeck, *Geschichte des Untergangs der antiken Welt* (4th ed.; Berlin, 1897-1921), I, 346, 381.

[38] E.g., E. Cavaignac, "Notes de demographie antique," *Journ. de la Soc. de statistique de Paris*, Jan., 1935, cited by Landry, *op. cit.*, p. 29, n. 1. Delbrück and Beloch both believe in a rise in population to the early third century, see note 11, above), but in my opinion they underestimate the effects of the plague of the late second century, the effects of urbanization on the birth rate, and other factors.

[39] This seems to be the opinion of M. I. Rostovtzeff, *Social and Economic History of the Roman Empire* (Oxford: Clarendon Press, 1926), in view of his remarks on the rapid economic decline under the late Severi in Chap. IX. See especially p. 489, n. 3, and pp. 504-5 of his third, Italian, edition. Rostovtzeff, however, vigorously challenges the idea that general depopulation had begun within the Empire before the Severi, although he admits that such was the case for Italy and Greece (pp. 429-30).

[40] This is the opinion of Seeck, *op. cit.*, I, Bk. II, Chap. 5, "Die Entvölkerung des Reiches," pp. 337 ff. It is supported with strong additional arguments and some corrections by Landry, *op. cit.*, pp. 1-33. See also A. Calderini, *I Severi: la crisi del impero nel III secolo* (Bologna: Cappelli, 1949), Chap. v, "La Crisi degli uomini, I. Diminuzione della popolazione," pp. 473-74; and G. Gigli, *op. cit.*, Chap. VII, "Regresso demografico," where the various factors causing the enfeeblement and decline are treated in detail. A. Grenier, "La Gaule romaine," in *Economic Survey of Ancient Rome*, III, Pt. IV (1937), 574-75, also believes that the decline had become well established by the time of the Severi. So, apparently, Alföldi in *Camb. Anc. Hist.* (Cambridge [Eng.]: Cambridge Univ. Press, 1932-39), XII, 164. E. Albertini, *L'Empire romain* (Paris: F. Alcan, 1929), pp. 304-5, speaks of the depopulation which had affected the central areas in the first and second centuries, extending to the periphery in the third. Surprisingly enough, M. Besnier, *L'Empire romain de l'avènement des Sévères au concile de Nicée* (Paris: Les Presses Univ. de France, 1937), does not deal with population conditions prior to 268, and H. M. D. Parker, *A History of the Roman World from A.D. 138 to 337* (London: Methuen and Co., 1935), virtually ignores the problem.

[41] Landry, *op. cit.*, pp. 4-5. On the unusually high death rate among imperial slaves, Burn, *op. cit.*, p. 9.

[42] *Ibid.;* Seeck, *op. cit.*, i, 364, 377.

[43] Ulpian's phrase *necessitas penuriae hominum* (*Dig.* 50. 6. 2. 1) refers to the class of municipal decurions.

[44] Not only in Italy, but also in the provinces, Dio lxxi. ii. 4; *Historia Augusta, Vita Marci* 22. 2.

[45] He recovered 100,000 captives from the Quadi and Marcomanni, Dio lxxii. 16.

[46] On the other hand, Russell suggests that urbanization gradually reduced the rate of population increase in the Empire until it started general depopulation, which in turn produced economic depression, *op. cit.*, p. 169, n. 3.

[47] P. 11 and notes 28, 29.

[48] See, for example, the statement of Cyprian on the shortage of manpower in agriculture, among sailors, and for the army (*Ad Demetrianum* 3), which Rostovtzeff (*op. cit.*, p. 489, n. 3) regards as too explicit to be rejected.

[49] Calderini, *op. cit.*, p. 473.

[50] For detailed treatments of this period, see Rostovtzeff, *op. cit.*, Chap. xi; Albertini, *op. cit.*, pp. 283-319; *Camb. Anc. Hist.*, xii, Chaps. ii-vi; and other general works on Roman history, such as those of Besnier and Parker cited above, n. 40.

[51] For Rostovtzeff, depopulation became the salient social and economic feature of the period, *op. cit.*, p. 551. Albertini considers shortages of men and money the two chief aspects of the crisis of the third century, *op. cit.*, pp. 304-5. It is surprising to find this important question passed over by F. Oertel in *Camb. Anc. Hist.*, xii, Chap. vii, "The Economic Life of the Empire."

[52] E.g., Jones, *op. cit.*, pp. 14-15.

[53] Landry, *op. cit.*, p. 18.

Supplementary Note

In a severely critical analysis of the character and types of evidence available, F. G. Meyer has recently demonstrated beyond all question that it is quite impossible to calculate with even approximate exactness the population of the city of Rome in ancient times ("Römische Bevölkerungsgeschichte und Inschriftenstatistik," *Historia*, ii (1954), 318-51.

II

[1] For more detailed treatments of these disorders, see the authorities cited in Chap. I, n. 50.

[2] Tacitus *Hist.* i. 64-69; ii. 12, 13, 56. On the depredations of soldiers in the third century, see Rostovtzeff, *Social and Economic History of the Roman Empire*, pp. 422-23.

[3] On requisitions for military purposes, see Rostovtzeff, *ibid.*, Chap. XI *passim*.

[4] See the list of inroads in A. Blanchet, *Les Trésors de monnaies romaines et les invasions germaniques en Gaule* (Paris, 1900), pp. 1-30. See also C. Jullian, *Histoire de la Gaule* (Paris, 1914), IV, Chaps. XIV, XV, XVI; and I. J. Manley, *Effects of the Germanic Invasions of Gaul 234-284 A.D.* (Berkeley: Univ. Calif. Press, 1934), Chap. II.

[5] *Camb. Anc. Hist.*, XII, 154-56, 298-99; Zosimus *Hist.* i. 37.

[6] *Camb. Anc. Hist.*, XII, 154-57, 309, 315; F. Stählin, *Die Schweiz in römischer Zeit* (Basel: B. Schwabe and Co., 1931), pp. 253-56.

[7] *Camb. Anc. Hist.*, XII, 300. For Gaul, see Manley, *op. cit.*, Chap. IV. See also Chap. III, below.

[8] Ammianus Marcellinus xxix. 12. 1; *Camb. Anc. Hist.*, XII, 160.

[9] On the depredations of the barbarians, see Jullian, *op. cit.;* the authors cited in Chap. I, n. 50; and *Camb. Anc. Hist.*, XII, 161. A good example is found in Amm. Marcel. xxiv. 12. 1, cited above. See also the frequent mention of recovery of Roman captives by various emperors, e.g., Zosimus i. 67. 3, *Hist. Aug., Vita Probi* 14. 6, 15. 5.

[10] For Gaul in particular, see Jullian, *op. cit.*, IV, 603; Grenier, "La Gaule romaine," pp. 578, 595.

[11] On the great pestilence of the third century, see the contemporary account of Cyprian *De mortalitate* 14, 16; *in Demetrianum* 10, 11; and Pontius *Vita Cypriani* 9. The following extracts offer testimony as to its universality: "There was hardly a Roman province, a city, a dwelling which was not seized and emptied by that universal pestilence," Orosius *Historiae* 7. 21. 4. "Not less than the war which raged on all sides, did the plague, attacking both towns and villages, destroy what was left of the human race, having never before in past times caused

such a loss of human beings," Zosimus i. 26; cf. i. 37. "And also a pestilence at that time fell upon the lands, starting from Ethiopia and spreading to almost every country both eastern and western, it emptied many cities of their inhabitants, and lasted fifteen years," Zonaras *Annals* 12. 21. Actually, it can be traced for nearly twenty years, for it began about 251 and was still active in 268. For other references, see the list quoted by Mary L. Hannan, *Thasci Caecili Cypriani de Mortalitate, A Commentary, with Introduction and Translation* (Washington, D. C.: Catholic Univ. of America, 1933), pp. 13-19. G. Sticker, *Abhandlungen aus der Seuchengeschichte und Seuchenlehre* (Giessen, 1908-12), I, 1, does not believe that this epidemic can be identified with any known to modern medical science, but A. Zinsser, *Rats, Lice and History* (Boston: Little, Brown and Co., 1935), p. 140, thinks that it included several distinct diseases, among which bubonic plague was dominant.

[12] Zosimus i. 71. 2. This recalls the similar rebellion of the Marcomanni colonized in North Italy under Marcus Aurelius, who took up arms and attacked Ravenna, Cassius Dio lxxii. 11. 4. For other possible revolts under Probus, see *Vita Probi* 17. 2.

[13] In Liguria, *Hist. Aug., Vita Proculi* 12. 1-3; Sicily, *ibid., Vita Gallieni* 4. 9. On brigandage in general, see Rostovtzeff, *op. cit.,* p. 620, n. 17.

[14] Grenier, *op. cit.,* pp. 564-65, 567, 578; Jullian, *op. cit.,* IV, 603.

[15] Albertini, *L'Empire romain,* pp. 304-5; Gigli, *La Crisi dell'impero romano,* p. 174.

[16] See the list of barbarian settlements in Seeck, *Geschichte des Untergangs der römischen Welt,* I, Anhang, p. 592.

[17] *Hist. Aug., Vita Aurel.* 48. 2.

[18] Since Dacia was not highly developed industrially and commercially, the bulk of its Romanized population must have been agriculturalists.

[19] *Vita Probi* 15. 2, 18. 21; Zosimus i. 68. 3, 71. 1, 2; Gigli, *op. cit.,* p. 174.

[20] *Vita Probi* 18.

[21] If, as seems to be the case, this was a whole tribe and not merely prisoners captured in battle, the number may not be hopelessly exaggerated since it would mean only some 25,000 men of military age. Even if the number is reduced by one-

half, it would mean a sensible addition to the local population and would indicate that a serious depletion of the latter had taken place.

[22] *Vita Probi* 21. 2.

[23] On these internal wars and barbarian invasions see the general histories of the Late Roman Empire, in particular, Seeck, *op. cit.,* Bde. I, 4, 5, 6; *Camb. Anc. Hist.,* Vol. XII; *Camb. Med. Hist.* (New York: Macmillan Co., 1911-36), Vol. I; Stein, *Geschichte des spätrömischen Reiches,* Vol. I; Besnier, *L'Empire romain;* Piganiol, *L'Empire chrétien.*

[24] *Natural History,* 18. 7. 35: *latifundia Italiam perdidere, iam vero et provincias.*

[25] On the growth and operation of these estates, see Frank, *Economic Survey of Ancient Rome,* V, 168-84, who discounts Pliny's statement cited above; Rostovtzeff, *op. cit.,* p. 69 and *passim;* Heitland, *Agricola* (Cambridge [Eng.]: Cambridge Univ. Press, 1920), pp. 203-385; M. Weber, *Die römische Agrargeschichte* (Stuttgart, 1891), Chap. IV. On conditions in Britain in the Late Empire, see R. G. Collingwood, "Roman Britain," *Economic Survey of Ancient Rome,* ed. by T. Frank, III, 12-13; in Gaul for the same period, Grenier, *op. cit.,* pp. 495-98, 633; Jullian, *op. cit.,* VIII, 130-46. For the Western Empire in general, S. Dill, *Roman Society in the Last Century of the Western Empire* (London, 1899), Bk. III, Chap. 2, "The Decay of the Middle Class and the Aggrandizement of the Aristocracy."

[26] On the transformation of the *coloni* into agricultural serfs, see the later discussion in this chapter. On free, itinerant laborers, see Jullian, *op. cit.,* p. 165.

[27] For the most recent discussion of the character of this much debated reform, see W. Seston, *Dioclétien et le tétrarchie* (Paris: E. de Boccard, 1946), I, 261-94, who reviews the earlier literature.

[28] *De mortibus persecutorum* 7. 2.

[29] *Caesares* 39. 32. This view finds support in Themistius *Orationes* viii. 113, where the orator declares that the taxes had doubled in the forty years preceding the accession of Valens in 364.

[30] For details see Seeck, in *Pauly-Wissowa, Real-Encyclopädie* VI, 1, 30-33 *s.v.* "epibole"; Piganiol, *op. cit.,* pp. 283-84. The emperors Gratian, Valentinian, and Theodosius ordered: "Whenever a contracting farmer is found to be in possession of a farm,

his right to which is derived from the ownership of the state or of temples, he shall have joined to his land a less productive field and an increase in tax valuation shall be imposed," *Codex Theod.* x. 3. 4. (378?).

[31] See the remarks of Heitland, *op. cit.,* pp. 388-89.

[32] A good résumé of the abuses in collecting the land tax is to be found in Bloch, *L'Empire romain. Evolution et décadence,* pp. 270-75. See also Seeck, *op. cit.,* II, 267 ff. On the sufferings of the smaller farmers in Gaul, Amm. Marcel. xvi. 5. 14, 15 and xvii. 3; Salvian *De gubernatione Dei* v. 34-50. For abuses in assessment of the land tax, Lactantius *De mort. persec.* 22-23, probably with reference to the census of 307. This passage, however, appears highly exaggerated and should be used with great reserve, Heitland, *op. cit.,* pp. 420-22.

[33] On the spread of malaria, Gigli, *op. cit.,* p. 176; *Enciclopedia italiana,* 21, 987; W. H. S. Jones, *Dea Febris. A Study of Malaria in Ancient Italy.* (n.d.); and N. Toscanelli, *La malaria nell'antichità e la fine degli Etrusci* (Milan, 1927).

[34] The most authoritative work on economic conditions in Britain of the Late Empire is R. G. Collingwood's "Roman Britain."

[35] On this point see Collingwood, *ibid.,* pp. 112-13, against those who assume a regular export trade in wheat from the island to the continent.

[36] *Panegyrici Veteres* vi. 9; Piganiol, *op. cit.,* p. 5.

[37] The fundamental studies on Gaul under the Late Empire are those of A. Grenier, "La Gaule romaine," and C. Jullian, *Histoire de la Gaule.* There is also much to be found in the older work of S. Dill, *Roman Society in the Last Century of the Western Empire.* All three have been cited already.

[38] Grenier, *op. cit.,* Chap. v, also Chap. vi, pp. 592-93; Jullian, *op. cit.,* Vol. vii, Chap. i.

[39] On life in Gaul as depicted by these writers, Dill, *op. cit.,* pp. 149-50, 167, 176 ff., 191, 227; Jullian, *op. cit.,* pp. 127-46, 183-88. Ausonius' *Mosella* was written during the recovery which followed Valentinian's pacification of the Rhine frontier in 368.

[40] Schanz-Hosius-Kruger, *Geschichte der lateinischen Literatur*

(Munich, 1907-20), IV, 2, 125-26. The reference to high prices seems of itself to indicate a serious shortage of production.

[41] *Incerti panegyricus Constantio Caesari dictus* (*Panegyrici Latini* viii [v], ed. Baehrens, 1911) 9. 21; *Incerti panegyricus Constantino Augusto dictus* (*Panegyr.* vi [vii]) 6. 2; *Mamertini genethliacus maximiano Augusto dictus* (*Panegyr.* xi [iii]) 15. 3; *Eumenii pro instaurandis scholis oratio* (*Panegyr.* ix [iv]) 18. 4; all cited and commented on by Grenier, *op. cit.*, pp. 592-99, who properly discounts the exaggerated statements of such examples of oratorical flattery.

[42] *Panegyr.* v (viii). 5. 4-5, 6. 1-5, 11. 1-4, 13. 1; Grenier, *op. cit.*, 602-6.

[43] *Panegyr.* v (viii). 6.

[44] Jullian, *op. cit.*, VIII, 175-76, 180-82. Cf. Ausonius *Epist.* xiv. 22-25.

[45] H. Schiller, *Geschichte der römischen Kaiserzeit* (Gotha, 1887), 2, 306; Grenier, *op. cit.*, p. 614.

[46] Schiller, *op. cit.*, pp. 376-90; Stählin, *op. cit.*, pp. 283-304.

[47] J. B. Bury, *The Invasion of Europe by the Barbarians*, pp. 281-83; L. Halphen, *Les Barbares* (2d ed.; Paris: F. Alcan, 1930), pp. 3-49.

[48] See p. 30.

[49] Amm. Marcel. xxxi. 6. 5-7; Zosimus v. 22. 6; Jullian, *op. cit.*, pp. 180, 238.

[50] For example, the Alemanni in 368, Amm. Marcel. xxvii. 10. 1-2. Cf. *Cod. Theod.* v. 7. 1 (366) and 2 (408 or 409) on the problem of recovered captives. Release of Gallic captives, Stählin, *op. cit.*, 287, citing Eunapius.

[51] See p. 37 for Julian's resort to British wheat. Ausonius *Epist.* xxvi. 9-15, 41-44; *Domestica* i. 27.

[52] Seeck, *op. cit.*, I, 409-14; Jullian, *op. cit.*, pp. 236-41. It is worth noting that from about the year 370, the Romanized population was forbidden to intermarry with the barbarians, so that any stimulus to the reproduction rate from this source was eliminated, *Cod. Theod.* iii. 14. 1 (370 or 373). On the date see Piganiol, *op. cit.*, p. 173, n. 25.

[53] The account given by Salvian about 440 seems to offer conclusive proof of a decrease in the agricultural class (*De guber-*

natione dei v. 21, 24, 28). Also, the comments of Grenier, *op. cit.*, pp. 620-23, bear out this conclusion. For the progressive depopulation, Beloch, "Die Bevölkerung Europas im Mittelalter," *Zeitschr. Socialwiss.*, 3 (1900), 406-7.

[54] One must not, of course, exaggerate the numbers of the barbarian settlers, as was done by ancient and many modern historians, see Bury, *op. cit.*, p. 42; Lot, *Le fin du monde antique* (Paris: Renaissance du livre, 1927), p. 267. On the character of the settlement, Halphen, *op. cit.*, pp. 24-26.

[55] R. Heuberger, *Ratien im Altertum und Frühmittelalter* (Innsbruck: Universitäts Verlag, 1932), I, 120-21; "Raetia," *RE*, I, 53, 58-61; Stählin, *op. cit.*, pp. 251 ff.; F. Wagner, *Die Römer in Bayern* (Munich: Knorr and Hirth, 1924), pp. 24-26.

[56] "Sardinia," *RE*, II, 2490, 2492; C. Belliani, *Sardegna e gli Sardi nella civiltà del mondo antico*, I (1928), II (1931). On the grain taxes, see Belliani, *ibid.*, I, 135-47.

[57] On the latifundia and the imperial domains, Belliani, *ibid.*, pp. 272-73, 309-11. The population of the island was never very great in ancient times and methods of production remained primitive, *ibid.*, pp. 276-86.

[58] *Ibid.*, pp. 276-86.

[59] *Cod. Theod.* ii. 25. 1 (725?). The agricultural labor on these domain lands was furnished by slaves who were permitted to marry and raise families. The distribution of these estates in hereditary leaseholds among numerous landholders is an indication of their having fallen out of cultivation, Belliani, *op. cit.*, II, 45-47.

[60] *Ibid.*, I, 285.

[61] *Cod. Theod.* xi. 7. 7 (353).

[62] *Ibid.*, viii. 5. 16.

[63] Wheat, Salvian *De gubernatione* vi. 68; pork and mutton, *Nov. Val.* xxxvi (452), with the comments of Belliani, *op. cit.*, p. 297. The *Expositio, ca.* 67, describes Sardinia as "very rich in crops and cattle," but this may safely be regarded as an exaggerated generalization.

[64] V. Scramuzza, "Roman Sicily," in *Economic Survey of Ancient Rome*, ed. by T. Frank, III, Pt. iii, 373. Scramuzza's survey virtually concludes with the third century.

[65] B. Pace, *Arte e civiltà della Sicilia antica* (Milan: Albrighi, Segati et Cie, 1949), IV, 219, 223. For the estates, Scramuzza, *op. cit.*, pp. 363-67.

[66] Salvian *De gubernatione* vi. 68; *Expositio, ca.* 66; Pace, *op. cit.*, IV, 219, 231; Scramuzza, *op. cit.*, pp. 349-52.

[67] Pace, *op. cit.*, pp. 140, 219. See also G. Salvioli, "Lo Stato e la popolazione d'Italia prima e dopo le invasioni barbariche," *Atti d. R. Acad. di scienze, letteri e belle arti di Palermo,* ser. 3, 5 (Palermo, 1900), 57 ff., cited by Pace.

[68] *Ca.* 59; also for horses, Symmachus iv. 58. Diocletian's *Edict of Prices* lists pork and wool, iv. 8, xxv. 3. In general, D. D. Van Nostrand, "Roman Spain," in *Economic Survey of Ancient Rome,* III, Pt. ii, 218.

[69] Avienus *Ora Maritima,* ll. 438-43.

[70] See Piganiol, *op. cit.*, p. 9.

[71] Piganiol, *ibid.*, n. 4.

[72] R. A. Haywood, "Roman Africa," in *Economic Survey of Ancient Rome,* Vol. IV, Pt. i, Chap. 3; Piganiol, *op. cit.*, p. 10.

[73] *Expositio, ca.* 61, wine, oil, cattle; Symmachus *Epist.* iv. 54, 74, grain; Piganiol, *op. cit.*, pp. 9-10.

[74] Berber raids and massacres of the peasants, Amm. Marcel. xxvii. 9, xxviii. 6; official corruption, Seeck, *op. cit.*, II³, 107-10; Piganiol, *op cit.*, pp. 181-82; revolt of Firmus, Amm. Marcel. xxix. 5; revolt of Gildo, Seeck, "Gildo," *RE,* VII, 360-61; F. Martroye, *Genséric, la conquête vandale en Afrique et la destruction de l'empire d'occident* (Paris, 1907), pp. 29-30, 34-36.

[75] C. Saumague, "Ouvriers agricoles ou rodeurs de celliers? Les circumcellions d'Afrique," *Ann. d'hist. econ. et soc.,* VI (1934), 351-64; Piganiol, *op. cit.*, p. 10. See also Martroye, *op. cit.*, pp. 7, 19, 37.

[76] *Cod. Theod.* xi. 28. 13. The figures for Africa Proconsularis are 9200 *centuriae* 141 *iugera* able to pay taxes, 5700 *centuriae* 144½ *iugera* untilled; for Byzacena, 7460 *centuriae* 180 *iugera* under cultivation, 7615 *centuriae* 3½ *iugera* unproductive. See Hayward, *op. cit.*, p. 118.

[77] Symmachus *Epist.* ii. 22.

[78] Sidonius Apollinaris *Epist.* i. 5. See pp. 35-36.

[79] Ambrose *Epist.* 39; Symmachus *Epist.* v. 12 (396?).

[80] *Ca.* 54.

[81] *Cod. Theod.* xiv. 4. 3 (363), 4. 4 (367); *Nov. Val.* xxxvi (452).

[82] For a detailed account of the Visigoths in Italy, see T. Hodgkin, *Italy and her Invaders* (Oxford, 1892), Vol. I, Pt. 2.

[83] *Cod. Theod.* xi. 28. 2.

[84] Amm. Marcel. xxviii. 5. 13.

[85] *Epist.* vi. 64

[86] For various views, see Seeck, "Colonatus," in *RE,* IV, I, 482-510; Rostovtzeff, *Studien zur Geschichte des römischen Kolonats* (Leipzig and Berlin, 1910); Rostovtzeff, "The Problem of the Origin of Serfdom in the Roman Empire," *Journ. Land and Public Utility Econ.,* 2 (1926), 198-207; Piganiol, *op. cit.,* pp. 276-79, with citation of the recent literature.

[87] *Cod. Theod.* v. 17. 1 (332).

[88] Bloch, *op. cit.,* p. 283.

[89] *Cod. Theod.* v. 17. 1.

[90] *Coloni* concealed or enticed away by new patrons, *Cod. Theod.* v. 17. 2 (386), 17. 3; iv. 23. 1 (400). *Coloni* and military service, *Codex Justinianus* i. 3. 16 (409); *Nov. Val.* xiii. 8 (445). *Coloni* and the clergy, *Cod. Just.* i. 3. 16 (409). *Coloni* and other hereditary occupation groups, *Cod. Theod.* xii. 19. 2 (400). In general, Seeck, *op. cit.,* 504-5.

[91] *Cod. Theod.* v. 18. 1 (419); *Nov. Val.* xxvii. 4 (449), xxxi (451); Seeck, *op. cit.,* 505.

[92] I agree with the definition of *inquilinus* given by Piganiol, *op. cit.,* pp. 278-79. For their change in status, *Cod. Just.* xi. 48. 6 (366); *Cod. Theod.* x. 12. 2 (368?); *Cod. Just.* xi. 53. 1 (371); *Cod. Theod.* v. 18. 1 (419).

[93] *Cod. Theod.* x. 12. 2 (368?); Piganiol, *op. cit.,* p. 276.

[94] On slavery in the Late Empire in general, W. L. Westermann, "Sklaverei," *RE,* Supplb., VI (1935), 1063-68. See also Piganiol, *op. cit.,* pp. 275-76, 404-6.

[95] When a new tenant took over a vacant holding on an imperial estate, he received a corresponding number of slaves attached to the estate, if these were available, *Cod. Theod.* ii. 25. 1 (334).

[96] For example, *Cod. Just.* vi. 1. 1 (286), 3 (317-23), 4 (317), 6 (332); *Cod. Theod.* x. 12. 1 (368-73), 2 (368-73).

[97] *Cod. Theod.* xiv. 18.

[98] On the existence of these peasant proprietors in the Late Empire, Piganiol, *op. cit.,* pp. 279, 280; citing *Cod. Theod.* iii. 1. 6 (391).

[99] These peasant proprietors are among those referred to in a law of 392 (*Cod. Theod.* x. 17. 3) which begins: "If the necessity of the public treasury should compel any person oppressed with an intolerable burden of debts (i.e. unpaid taxes) to sell his own property ..."; cf. *ibid.,* v. 11. 11 (386).

[100] See the titles of sections in the Codes of Theodosius II and Justinian: *Cod. Theod.* v. 15, *de omni agro deserto et quando steriles fertilibus imponantur;* x. 8, *de bonis vacantibus; Cod. Just.* xi. 19, *de omni agro,* and the like; x. 10, *de bonis,* and the like; *Nov. Anthem.* iii, *de bonis vacantibus.* In addition, for vacant lands on imperial estates, *Cod. Just.* xi. 62, 3, 5. 7. There was always more than enough unoccupied land available for distribution to veterans, *Cod. Theod.* vii. 20. 3 (320), 8 (364), 11 (373). The *epibole* was universal, x. 3. 4 (383).

[101] *Cod. Theod.* v. 11. 6 and 7 (365).

[102] *Ibid.,* 13. 4.

[103] *Ibid.,* 13. 30. See also v. 13. 34 (394), and v. 12. 32 (434), where the conditions of occupation are made still more favorable.

[104] *Ibid.,* v. 11. 12.

[105] *Ibid.,* 8.

[106] Constantine I had to remit back taxes to Autun in 311, *Panegyr.* v (viii). 10. 5, 13. 1; Julian lowered the rate of the land tax for all Gaul, Amm. Marcel. xvi. 5. 14. *Cod. Theod.* xi. 28, *de indulgentiis debitorum* contains seventeen constitutions dated between 363 and 438, most of which indicate cancellations of delinquent land taxes. *Ibid.,* v. 12. 32 (434) refers to an important general remission. Later indulgences of this kind were authorized by *Nov. Val.* xiii (445); *Nov. Marcian.* ii (450) and ii (458), in which a distressing account of the condition of the small landholders is given. Of course, some of these remissions came in the wake of civil wars and invasions. But that was by no means true of all cancellations nor of many of the areas given this sort of relief.

[107] *Cod. Theod.* v. 12. 14-32.

[108] *Ibid.,* vi. 2. 14. Possibly as a result of invasions in these provinces. For the *collatio glebalis,* see Seeck, *RE,* iv, 1, 365-67.

[109] *Cod. Theod.* vi. 2. 15.

[110] *Ibid.*, v. 13. 33.

[111] *Ibid.*, vi. 3. 4.

[112] *Ibid.*, 2. 24. This applies to properties taken over under a tax-equalizing process, the *sors peraequationis.*

[113] This phrase occurs in *Nov. Val.* xiii. 8 (445).

III

[1] Chap. I, p. 17 ff. and notes.

[2] Chap. II, p. 23 ff.

[3] See Chap. II, n. 11, for the references in ancient writers who emphasize the losses incurred by the towns.

[4] Chap. I, pp. 19-20.

[5] *Camb. Anc. Hist.,* XII, 264.

[6] M. I. Rostovtzeff, *Social and Economic History of the Roman Empire,* pp. 358-80; *Camb. Anc. Hist.,* XII, 264-65; Calderini, *I Severi: la crisi dell'impero nel III secolo,* pp. 473-74.

[7] On the barbarians' lack of success in attacking well-fortified cities, see *Camb. Anc. Hist.,* XII, 160; cf. Chap. II, p. 25.

[8] A. Blanchet, *Les Trésors de monnaies romaines et les invasions germanique en Gaule,* pp. 1-30; Grenier, "Gaule romaine," pp. 576-78, 599; I. J. Manley, *Effects of the Germanic Invasions of Gaul, 234-284 A.D.,* pp. 91-103.

[9] See Chap. II, p. 25 and note 9; Manley, *op. cit.*

[10] On the disappearance of the commercial middle class and the small craftsmen in the towns of Gaul, see Grenier, *op. cit.,* p. 599. In general, Rostovtzeff, *op. cit.,* p. 411, and Chap. XI *passim.*

[11] Collingwood, "Roman Britain," pp. 11-12.

[12] Blanchet, *Les Enceintes romaines de la Gaule* (Paris, 1907), pp. 283-86. Some, like Aventicum (Avenches), were never rebuilt.

[13] Grenier, *op. cit.,* p. 599. Cf. Bloch, *L'Empire romain. Evolution et décadence,* p. 255. Manley, *op. cit.,* p. 76, has doubts about depopulation as the explanation of this shrinkage, but without good reasons.

[14] Ammianus was in Gaul during the years 354-57. His description of contemporary Gaul is found in Book XV. 11.

[15] Cap. 58. The author's remark about Treves, *"ubi et habitare dominus dicitur,"* clearly indicates that he lacked first-hand knowledge of the city.

[16] *Ordo urb. nobil.* vi, x, xviii, xix.

[17] F. Koepp, *Die Römer in Deutschland* (Bielefeld, 1912), pp. 126-30; Rau, "Treveri," *RE,* A 6, 2, 2320-53. For its decline in the fifth century, Salvian *De gubernatione Dei* vi. 75 ff. For the mint, *Not. Dign. Occ.* (ed. Seeck), xi. 44; for the *gynaecia, ibid.,* xi. 58; for *fabricae, ibid.,* ix. 37 f.

[18] *Expositio,* cap. 58; Grenier, *op. cit.,* p. 585; L. A. Constans, *Arles antique* (Paris: E. de Boccard, 1921), particularly pp. 97-105; F. Lot, *Recherches sur la population et la superficie des cités remontant à la période gallo-romane.* Pt. I (Paris: Lib. Ancienne Honoré Champion, 1945), pp. 166-67. About 400, owing to the exposed position of Treves, Arles supplanted it as the residence of the praetorian prefect of Gaul. It also had a mint and imperial factories, *Not. Dign. Occ.* ix. 43; xi. 54, 75.

[19] See Lot, *op. cit.,* pp. 336-37. I have adopted his interpretation of Ausonius, *Ordo urb. nobil.* xviii.

[20] Blanchet, *op. cit.,* pp. 283-86; Lot, *op. cit.,* p. 311.

[21] This is not contradicted by the appearance of imperial workshops of several kinds in the cities of Gaul. Including those at Arles and Treves, the *Notitia Dignitatum* (*Occ.* ix and xi) lists six silk works, one linen factory, two dyeing establishments, three workshops for decorating arms and armor, and nine arsenals for the manufacture of weapons and armor of various sorts. But as will be seen in a later chapter, the presence of these government industries is not so much an indication of urban growth as a testimony to the decline of privately operated enterprises and to an inadequate supply of skilled labor. Cf. Grenier, *op. cit.,* pp. 638-39.

[22] For barbarian raids of the fourth century, see Blanchet, *op. cit.,* p. 355; A. Blanchet, *Les Rapports entre les depots monetaires et les événements militaires, politiques et economiques* (Paris, 1936), pp. 61-66; Amm. Marcel. 16. 3. 1, on the Rhineland towns in 356; Chap. II, pp. 30, 41.

[23] Grenier, *op. cit.,* pp. 614-23, 632-42.

[24] *Ordo urb. nobil.* xi-xiv.

[25] Van Nostrand, "Roman Spain," p. 219; Piganiol, *L'Empire chrétien,* p. 4; Schulten, "Hispania," *RE,* VIII, 2044-46.

[26] There were imperial dye works on the Baleares Is., *Not. Dign. Occ.* 11. 71. Exports to Gaul, Ausonius, *op. cit.,* xix, 18. Spanish linen, Piganiol, *op. cit.* For the ruinous condition of many Spanish towns, Ausonius *Epist.* xxix. 58-59; xxx. 221-38.

[27] See the summary account in R. M. Haywood, "Roman Africa," Chap. III.

[28] *Ibid.,* p. 115.

[29] C. E. Van Sickle, "The Public Works of Africa in the Reign of Diocletian," *Class. Phil.,* xxv (1930), 173-79; Haywood, *op. cit.,* p. 119.

[30] *Cod. Theod.* xiii. 4. 1 (334).

[31] Orosius vii. 33. 5; cf. Amm. Marcel. xxix. 5. 17. Sabratha in Tripolitana had been destroyed in a great raid of the Garamantes in 363, Amm. Marcel. xxviii. 6. It was not rebuilt.

[32] E.g., Frank, *Economic Survey of Ancient Rome,* v, 297; Rostovtzeff, *op. cit.,* p. 183; Albertini, *L'Empire romain,* pp. 129-32.

[33] This applies in particular to the towns of the peninsula. It is borne out by excavations at Minturnae (J. Johnson, "Minturnae," *RE,* Suppl. Bd. vii, 490); G. Calza, "Ostia," *RE,* xvii, 2, 1663; and Cosa. Cosa was virtually abandoned late in the Republican period and experienced no recovery even under the Principate. Its fate was typical of other cities of the Etruscan coastal area. The temples and *capitolium* were abandoned in the third century (F. E. Brown, "Cosa I, History and Topography," *Mem. Amer. Acad. Rome,* xx [1951], 7-113). Later excavations have revealed a very limited occupation in the fourth century.

[34] In L. Friedlaender, *Darstellungen aus der Sittengeschichte Roms* . . . , iv, 19-20. When these lectures were written I had not had the opportunity of consulting the interesting work of S. Mazzarino, *Aspetti sociali del quarto secolo* (Rome: L'Erma di Bretschneider, 1951) in which Chapter v, "Aspetti del problema demografico," is devoted largely to the question of the population of Rome in the fourth and fifth centuries. On the basis of statements in *Cod. Theod.* xiv. 4. 4. (367) and *Nov. Val.* 36 (452), relating to the pork supply of Rome, Mazzarino calculates that the recipients of the dole in 367 numbered 317,333 and 141,120 in 452. Accordingly, he believes that in 367 Rome was fully as populous as at the time of Augustus. Admitting a

decline under the Severi, he nonetheless claims a great increase for the early fourth century and considers that the real decline was brought about by the sack of Rome by Alaric in 410, which he considers to have reduced the population by 44 per cent. In general, Mazzarino's interpretation of population change in the Late Empire is that the small towns and the rural areas suffered severe and continuous depopulation, whereas Rome, Constantinople, Alexandria, and a few other large cities experienced a great increase in the number of their inhabitants. I am thoroughly in accord with this view of the decline of the small towns and of the population of the countryside and readily concede a rapid growth for Constantinople, Milan, Treves, and Ravenna, which became imperial residences and administrative centers, but question any increase for Alexandria and cities like it and cannot accept a rise in the population of Rome. Its abandonment as a capital city and the removal of the court and the central government bureaus must have drawn off thousands of persons. Furthermore, the failure to replace its praetorian garrison and the dissolution of the urban cohorts, its main police force, early in the fourth century indicate a lessening of the danger of mob violence and a decrease in the criminal element quite inconsistent with the idea of a tremendous influx of strangers into the city. It is also difficult to explain such a great increase in the number of the recipients of the dole in view of the restrictions placed upon admission to the list of state pensioners. There must be some other interpretation of the data supplied in *Cod. Theod.* XIV. 4. 4 and *Nov. Val.* 36 than that offered by Mazzarino.

[35] *The End of the Ancient World,* p. 70. According to Graffunder, the population of Rome had sunk to between 30,000 and 40,000 by the time of Valentinian III (*RE,* 2d ser., I, 1060).

[36] Note 33, above.

[37] *Ordo urb. nobil.* viii.

[38] Ausonius, *ibid.,* ix; *Expositio,* cap. 56; *Not. Dign. Occ.* xi. 39, 49.

[39] Arsenals at Concordia, Ticenum, Verona, Mantua, Cremona, Luca (*Not. Dign. Occ.* ix. 22-27); *gynaecium* at Milan, *ibid.,* xi. 50; *linyficum* at Ravenna, *ibid.,* xi. 63.

[40] *Gynaecia* at Rome and Canusium in Apulia, *ibid.,* 51, 52; dye works at Tarentum, *ibid.,* xi. 64. On the small size of the

North Italian towns of the Late Empire, see Beloch, "Die Bevölkerung Italiens im Altertum," *Klio,* 3 (1903), 487.

[41] Urbanization of the Danubian-Illyrian area, J. Jung, *Grundriss der Geographie von Italien und dem Orbis Romanus, Handb. der kl. Altertumswissenschaft* (Munich, 1897), III, 3, 1, 132-35. Raetia, J. Egger, "Die Barbareneinfälle in die Provinz Rätien und deren Besetzung durch Barbaren," *Arch f. Osterreich. Gesch.,* 90 (1901), 102-5; "Raetia," *RE,* I², 58-61. E. Poleschek, "Noricum," *RE,* XVII, 1, 971-1048, particularly 995 and 1011-13. See also the special articles on Salonae, Spalatum, Sirmium, and Siscia in *RE. Fabricae, Not. Dign. Occ.* xi. 17-22; gynaecia, *ibid.,* xi. 46-48; mint at Siscia, *ibid.,* xi. 39.

Along with Sirmium, the *Expositio* (*ca.* 58) lists as a *civitas maxima,* Noricum, from which it derives the term *Norica vestis.* Here the province is mistaken for a city, but the reference to *vestis,* coupled with *Edict of Prices* (xix, 35, *byrrus Noricus;* 43, *banata Norike;* 44, *bedox Norikos*) indicates the manufacture and export of textiles. In Dalmatia, Solana (Salona) is described as *civitas splendida, Expositio* (*ca.* 53).

[42] For the history and administration of the dole in Rome, see Cardinali, "Frumentatio," in De Ruggiero, *Dizionario Epigrafico,* III, 214 ff.; M. I. Rostowzew, "Frumentum," *RE,* VII, 126 ff.; B. Kubler, "Panis civilis," *ibid.,* XVIII, 3, 606-11; J. P. Waltzing, *Étude historique sur les corporations professionelles chez les romains* (Louvain, 1896), II, 19-26; Frank, *op. cit.,* vol. v, *passim.*

[43] *Hist. Aug., Vita Severi* 18.3, 23.3; Besnier, *L'Empire romain,* pp. 35, 247; Fluss, "Severus," *RE,* II², 1994. The evidence of the *Vita* is open to challenge, but that is not of cardinal importance since the free distribution of oil was certainly a practice from the time of Aurelian. See note 44, following.

[44] See Domazewski, "L. Domitius Aurelianus," *RE,* v, 1397-98; Besnier, *op. cit.,* pp. 249-50.

[45] See the calculations of Kahrstedt in Friedlaender, *op. cit.,* IV, 9-10, 19-20, for the decline between Septimius Severus and Constantine I.

[46] On the shipowners *(navicularii),* Waltzing, *op. cit.,* pp. 6-58, 397-99; E. Kornemann, "Collegium," *RE,* IV, 380-480, particularly 444 ff.; A. Stoeckle, "Navicularii," *RE,* XVI, 2, 1899-1932. See also Rostovtzeff, *op. cit., passim.*

[47] Waltzing, *op. cit.,* pp. 398-408.

[48] *Pistores,* Waltzing, *op. cit.,* pp. 404-5; A. Hug, *RE,* 20², 1821-31; grain merchants *(negotiatores frumentarii),* Waltzing, *op. cit.,* pp. 402-3; oil merchants *(olearii), ibid.,* pp. 403-4; pork dealers *(suarii), ibid.,* pp. 405-6. Even the grain measurers *(mensores frumentarii)* enjoyed like privileges, *ibid.,* p. 405.

[49] Waltzing, *ibid.,* pp. 49, 256-57, 406-7. It is impossible to think of individual contracts in the case of the *fabri* or their associates, the *centenarii* and *dendropharii,* in so far as their obligation to serve as municipal fire brigades is concerned. This was an obligation imposed upon their colleges as such and would of necessity apply to all active members. In many instances, no doubt, permission to organize such corporations was contingent upon their undertaking the duty of fire fighting (see Pliny *Epist.* x. 33-34). In this sense Callistratus was right when he wrote that they had been organized to serve public needs (*Dig.* 50. 6. 6 [5] § 12), and their service was correctly interpreted as a *munus.* The extension of this concept in the early third century to cover the relations of members of other colleges who served the state under individual contracts is easy to understand (*Dig.* 50. 6. [5]. 3).

[50] Waltzing, *op. cit.,* pp. 407-8.

[51] Waltzing, *op. cit.,* pp. 259-348; Kornemann, *RE, IV,* 442-53; Stoeckle, *RE,* xvi, 2, 1913 ff.; Hug, *RE,* xx, 2, 1829 ff.

[52] *Cod. Theod.* xiii. 5, *de naviculariis.* There are also ten ordinances on the properties of shipowners, *ibid.,* 6, *de praediis naviculariorum;* and two on their ships, *ibid.,* 7, *de navibus non excusandis.*

[53] *Ibid.,* 5. 1. Law 6, of 334, mentions an ordinance which had organized the guild of *navicularii.*

[54] *Ibid.,* 5. 19.

[55] *Ibid.,* 5. 2. Cf. 6. 1 (326), etc.

[56] *Ibid.,* 5. 5, 7, 8, 9, 10.

[57] E.g., 5. 8 and 9.

[58] *Ibid.,* 5. 14.

[59] On the relation of the bakers *(pistores)* and the millers *(molendinarii),* see Waltzing, *op. cit.,* pp. 85-86. It is not known when the millers were organized as a separate corporation. They appear as a state-controlled corporation under Theodoric, *CIL* vi. 1711 (499). Water mills were known to the Romans from

the beginning of our era, but only came into general use from the fourth century, Hug, *RE,* xvi, 1, 1065-67. Mills in Rome used to prepare flour for the bread dole are mentioned in *Cod. Theod.* xiv. 15. 4 (398). They are presumably those located on the Janiculum; cf. Platner-Ashby, *Topographical Dictionary of Ancient Rome* (London: Oxford Univ. Press, 1929), p. 345.

[60] *Cod. Theod.* xiv. 3. 1 (319) ; cf. 5 (364).

[61] *Ibid.,* 3. 1, 3 (364), 13 (369).

[62] *Ibid.,* 3. 8 (365), 20 (398), 21 (417).

[63] *Ibid.,* 3. 2 (355), 12 (365), 14 (372). It was also found necessary to draft bakers every five years from Africa for service in Rome, *ibid.,* 3. 12 (365), 17 (380).

[64] *Ibid.,* ix. 40. 3 (319), 5, 6, and 7 (all of 364), 9 (368? 370?).

[65] *Ibid.,* xiv. 3. 10 (365?). On these pack drivers *(catabolenses),* see Waltzing, *op. cit.,* pp. 61-62; Seeck, *RE,* iii, 1782. Other corporations connected with the civic *annona* and similarly subject to state control were the measurers *(mensores frumentarii)* and the bargemen on the Tiber *(codicarii* or *caudicarii), Cod. Theod.* xiv. 2 (355), 15. 1 (364), 4. 9 (417). Also the *saccarii* or long-shoremen, for whose corporation Valentinian I sought recruits in 364, *ibid.,* 22. 1 (364). Cf. Waltzing, *op. cit.,* pp. 63-64, 69-72; Seeck, "codicarii," *RE,* iv, 173-74.

[66] *Cod. Theod.* xiv. 4. 1.

[67] *Ibid.*

[68] *Ibid.,* 4. 5 (389), 7 (397), 8 (408).

[69] *Ibid.,* 4. 10 (419). This ordinance united them with the *suarii,* but they are found forming separate corporations in 452, *Nov. Val.* iii. 35. 2. 8. On the importance of these three groups for the food supply of Rome, Symmachus *Relationes* (ed. Seeck) xiv. 3 (384-85).

[70] There is, unfortunately, a lack of specific information about them in the Late Empire. They are, however, almost certainly included in the *corporatos negotiores, membra aeternae urbis* of Symmachus *Rel.* xiv. 1. Some of them are mentioned more specifically later in the same document: *caupones et obsequia pistoria frugis et olei baiulos multosque id genus patriae servientes enumerare fastigium est* (xiv. 3). It is quite clear from the context that the reference is to the food dealers of Rome in general, and also that they all were organized into obligatory cor-

porations bound to pursue their trades under government control in the public interest. On the *caupones,* see Waltzing, *op. cit.,* p. 100; on the *frugis et olei baiuli, ibid.,* pp. 88-89; and for the corporation of the *susceptores vini, ibid.,* p. 98. Symmachus also states that the corporation of the *mancipes salinarum,* or salt concessionaires, had been reduced to so few members that they could not perform their public duties and consequently asked for the recall of deserters, *Rel.* 44 (384-85). On their identification with the *mancipes thermarum,* Waltzing, *op. cit.,* pp. 126, 426; Steinwenter, "Manceps," *RE,* xiv, 995-96.

[71] *Cod. Theod.* xiv. 2. 4 (412).

[72] Waltzing, *op. cit.,* p. 211.

[73] Grenier, *op. cit.,* p. 599.

[74] It was also called the *collatio lustralis* because it was collected once every five years. For details, see Seeck, "Collatio Lustralis" in *RE,* iv, 370-76 and *Cod. Theod.* xiii. 1. 1-21. On the role of the municipal colleges, see Waltzing, *op. cit.,* pp. 183-84, 191-93, 211.

[75] See note 49, above; Waltzing, *op. cit.,* pp. 203-5.

[76] Waltzing, *ibid.,* p. 271, n. 2.

[77] *Ibid.,* pp. 272-73.

[78] *Cod. Theod.* xiv. 8. 1 (315).

[79] *Ibid.,* 7. 1.

[80] *Ibid.,* xii. 19. 1. Cf. also laws 2 and 3 (400), which prescribe time limits of thirty and forty years within which *coloni* who have run off to enter corporations or municipal councils and, conversely, runaway *curiales* and *corporati* may be recalled to their inherited status.

[81] *Nov. Maiorian.* 7. 3 (458); *corporati* performing public services under the direction of the *curiales* are not to live outside their cities.

[82] *Cod. Theod.* xiii. 4. 1.

[83] *Ibid.,* 2; cf. laws 3 (344) and 4 (374). The latter specifies exemption from taxes and from forced services for professors of painting in Africa.

[84] *Ibid.,* 3, *de medicis et professoribus.*

[85] Amm. Marcel. xxviii. 4. 28; Symm. *Rel.* 6. 9.

[86] Actors (actresses), *Cod. Theod.* xiv. 3. 21 (403); xv. 7, *de scaenicis,* especially laws 1 (371), 2 (371), 4 (380), 8 (381),

9 (381), 13 (414). For religious and moral reasons, however, members of the theatrical profession were excused at times from their hereditary services. See, for example, *Cod. Theod.* xv. 7. 1, 2, 4, and 8; for charioteers, *ibid.*, xiv. 3. 21 (403), xv. 5. 3 (409), 7. 7 (381); for image bearers *(signiferi)* and banner carriers *(cantabrarii), ibid.*, xiv. 7. 2 (412); for fortunetellers *(nemesiaci* and *vitutiarii), ibid.* See, in general, Waltzing, *op. cit.*, pp. 135-39.

[87] On the municipal councilors, then regularly known as *decuriones,* of the Principate, see S. Dill, *Roman Society from Nero to Marcus Aurelius* (London, 1905), Chap. II; Rostovtzeff, *op. cit.;* Kübler, "Decurio," *RE,* IV, 2319-52.

[88] Rostovtzeff, *op. cit.*, pp. 183, 186, 190, 358, 367, 375, 398, 411-13.

[89] *Dig.* 50. 6. 2. 1.

[90] Note 73, above.

[91] For such exceptions, *Cod. Theod.* xiii. i. 4 (362). The minimum of 25 *iugera, ibid.*, xii. 1. 33 (342).

[92] Good accounts of the *curiales* of the Late Empire are found in S. Dill, *Roman Society in the Last Century of the Western Empire,* Bk. III, Chap. 2; Waltzing, *op. cit.*, pp. 215-17; Piganiol, *op. cit.*, pp. 356-58; Bloch, *op. cit.*, pp. 262-82; Kübler, *op. cit.*, 2343-50.

[93] *Nov. Maiorian.* 7. pr. (458).

[94] *Cod. Theod.* xii. 1, *de decurionibus.*

[95] *Ibid.*, 1. 1 (313), 10 (325), 11 (325), et cetera.

[96] *Ibid.*, 1. 7 (320), 20 (331).

[97] *Ibid.*, 1. 6 (319), et cetera.

[98] *Ibid.*, 1. 13.

[99] Sons of civil servants, *Cod. Theod.* xii. 1. 7 (320); soldiers and veterans, *ibid.*, 1. 32 (341), repeated in 1. 35 (343), 1. 89 (381); shirkers, *ibid.*, 1. 83 (380).

[100] Flight to imperial services, *Cod. Theod.* xii. 1. 10 (325), 13 (326), 22 (336), 94 (383), 161 (399), 168 (409); to monastic societies, *ibid.*, 1. 63 (370? 373?), referring to Egypt, *Nov. Val.* 34. 3 (452); to the colonate on large estates, *ibid.*, 1. 146 (395); to the protection of influential persons, *ibid.*, 1, 50. 2 (362); to various corporations, *ibid.*, 1. 62 (364), 81 (380); to the armed forces, *Cod. Theod.* vii. 2. 1 (383), 2 (385); to forests and un-

inhabited areas, Salvian, *De gubernatione dei* v. 21; to general flight, *Cod. Theod.* xii. 1. 143 (395), 144 (395), *Nov. Maiorian.* 7. 3 (458).

[101] The imperial policy in this matter changed from time to time, cf. *Cod. Theod.* xii. 1. 49 (361), 59 (364), 91 (382), 115 (386), 163 (399); *Nov. Maiorian.* 7. 7 (458), and so forth.

[102] *Cod. Theod.* xii. 1. 69 (365-73).

[103] Amm. Marcel. xxvii. 7. 7 (365). On the crushing burden of taxation and public services, *Nov. Maiorian.* 7. 3; Waltzing, *op. cit.,* p. 338. Refusal to marry and have children, *Nov. Just.* 38, pr. 1 (535), which also reveals the numerical decline and economic ruin of this class. Although later than the fall of the Empire in the West, this constitution may safely be considered to refer to conditions of long standing.

[104] *Nov. Maiorian.* 7. 3.

IV

[1] On the legions to 193, see H. M. D. Parker, *The Roman Legions* (Oxford: Clarendon Press, 1928); Ritterling, "Legio," *RE,* xii, 1348-62. For additions under the Severi, see H. M. D. Parker, "The Legions of Diocletian and Constantine," *J.R.S.,* xxiii (1935), 175-76; Besnier, *L'Empire romain* . . . , p. 38; and the list in Ritterling, *op. cit.*

[2] Tacitus *Ann.* iv. 5.

[3] G. L. Cheesman, *The Auxilia of the Roman Imperial Army* (Oxford, 1914), pp. 56, 168. See also H. M. D. Parker, "Auxilia," *Oxford Classical Dictionary,* who allows 130,000 for the time of Augustus and 225,000 for the second century.

[4] H. M. D. Parker, *History of the Roman World from A.D. 138 to 337* (London: Methuen and Co., 1936), p. 269, gives 300,000. A lesser figure is implied by those who accept this as the total at the death of Severus. See n. 5.

[5] Cheesman, *op. cit.,* p. 169, allows over 400,000; J. Carcopino, "Sur une statistique méconnue de l'armée romaine au debut du iii siècle après J. C.," *Mélanges Syriens offerts à M. Réne Dussaud* (Paris: P. Geuthner, 1939), i, 215, estimates 199,650

legionaries, 202,600 auxiliaries, in all 412,250 for the time of Septimius Severus. The figure of 300,000 is supported by Marquardt, *Handbuch der römischen Alterthümer* (Leipzig, 1881-88), II², 241; Grosse, *Römische Militärgeschichte von Gallienus bis zum Beginn der byzantinischen Themenverfassung* (Berlin: Weidmann, 1920), p. 253; Besnier, *op cit.*, p. 303; A. Segrè, "The *Annona Civica* and the *Annona Militaris*," *Byzantion*, XVI, 2 (1942-43), 431-33; it is implied in the calculations of other writers for the size of the army in 284. See below.

[6] Parker, "The Legions of Diocletian and Constantine," p. 176; Parker, *History of the Roman World*, pp. 270-71.

[7] So Mommsen, "Das römische Militärwesen seit Diocletian," *Hermes*, XXIV (1889), 257.

[8] E. Stein, *Geschichte des spätrömischen Reiches*, I, 76; M. Cary, *History of Rome Down to the Reign of Constantine* (London: Macmillan Co., 1938), p. 738; Seeck, *Geschichte des Untergangs der römischen Welt*, I⁴, 255, thinks 350,000 is a possible maximum, and Nischer apparently agrees, "Army Reforms," p. 11, cited in the next note.

[9] N. H. Baynes, "Three Notes on the Reforms of Diocletian and Constantine," *J.R.S.*, XV, 1925, following Mommsen and also Parker, "Legions of Diocletian and Constantine," p. 184, in opposition to E. v. Nischer's interpretation in "The Army Reforms of Diocletian and Constantine and Their Modifications," *J.R.S.*, XIII (1923), 1-53, repeated in J. Kromayer and G. Veith, *Heerwesen und Kriegsführung der Griechen und Römer, Handb. d. kl. Altertums Wissenschaft* (Munich: Beck, 1928), IV, 3, 2. The important work of D. van Berchem, *L'Armée de Dioclétien et la réforme constantinienne* (Paris: Imprimerie Nat., 1952), does not discuss the size of the reformed army.

[10] *De mort. persec.* 7. 2.

[11] Besnier, *op. cit.*, p. 305; Ensslin, *Camb. Anc. Hist.*, XII, 397; Segrè, *op. cit.*, p. 432; Grosse, *op. cit.*, p. 252; Ritterling, *op. cit.*, p. 1350.

[12] *De mens.* i. 7.

[13] So Nischer, *op. cit.*, p. 4.

[14] Stein, *op. cit.*, p. 76, favors the beginning; Segrè, on other grounds, reaches approximately the same number for the close, *op. cit.*, p. 433.

[15] Zosimus ii. 5. 1.

[16] Cf. Grosse, *op. cit.*, p. 253; Seeck, *op. cit.*, ii, Anhang, p. 480.

[17] Agath. v. 13. Possibly this includes the navy; cf. the 45,000 which Lydus gives as the strength of the navy under Diocletian (*De mens.* i. 7).

[18] E.g., Grosse, *op. cit.*, pp. 251-52; Ritterling, *op. cit.*, pp. 1350-52; Nischer, *op. cit.*, p. 53.

[19] Mommsen, *op. cit.;* Nischer, *Heerwesen*, pp. 581-82.

[20] Mommsen, *op. cit.*, pp. 256-58; Nischer, *op. cit.*, pp. 580-81; Delbrück, *Geschichte der Kriegskunst*, ii³, 270, 314.

[21] For the whole question see Nischer, *J.R.S.*, xiii, 1-53, and *Heerwesen*, pp. 482-85, 568-75.

[22] Nischer, in *Heerwesen*, p. 572.

[23] *L'Empire chrétien*, p. 331, based on Lydus *De mens.* i. 7.

[24] Seeck, *op. cit.*, i, Anhang, p. 480.

[25] *The End of the Ancient World and the Beginning of the Middle Ages*, pp. 70-71.

[26] Cary, *op. cit.*, p. 738; Grosse, *op. cit.*, p. 253; Stein, *op. cit.*, p. 107. All attribute the increase in this figure to Diocletian. Segrè, *op. cit.*, p. 433, allows less than 400,000 at the death of Diocletian, 500,000 under Diocletian. Besnier, *op. cit.*, p. 305, also favors 400,000 after Diocletian's reforms.

[27] *The Invasion of Europe by the Barbarians*, p. 41.

[28] Lot is the only one to differ appreciably in placing this at from 228,000 to 233,000. Nischer, in *Heerwesen*, p. 581, and Parker, *op. cit.*, p. 273, also accept approximately 200,000. Seston, *Diocletian et la tétrarchie*, i, 298, in discussing the enlargement under Diocletian does not commit himself to a definite figure, but does place the total at over twice that of earlier times. This seems to imply a number between 500,000 and 600,000.

[29] A. H. M. Jones, *Ancient Economic History*, p. 15, "a temporary decline."

[30] See Nischer, in *Heerwesen*, p. 581. Certainly, following the reorganization of Diocletian and Constantine, the eastern and western armies were under separate commands, and independent in matters of recruitment and supplies.

[31] Parker, *J.R.S.*, xxiii, 175 ff.

[32] Grosse, *op. cit.,* pp. 198-220; Ensslin, *op. cit.,* pp. 396-97.

[33] J. Vogt, *Constantin der Grosse und sein Jahrhundert* (Munich: Münchner Verlag, 1949), pp. 239-40.

[34] Nischer, for example, speaks of Diocletian's levies as having proved such a strain as almost to reach a breaking point ("Army Reforms," p. 19), but this judgment rests upon an exaggerated estimate of the new corps organized by that emperor. If the result was actually so devastating, it is further evidence for the sparseness of the total population.

[35] *De mort. persec.* 7. 2.

[36] Nischer, in *Heerwesen,* p. 484. Delbrück, however, allows only 15 per cent, *op. cit.,* p. 244.

[37] Nischer thinks it very doubtful that even Diocletian was able to man his new legions fully (*op. cit.,* p. 485) and considers the same to have been true of Constantine, after whom the number of effectives declined steadily ("Army Reforms," pp. 34, 35).

[38] For the system of recruitment in the Late Empire, see the studies of Mommsen, Seeck, Grosse, Nischer, and Piganiol cited above, and also Liebenam, "Dilectus," *RE,* v, 1, 629-38, in addition to *Cod. Theod.* vii. 1 *de re militare;* 13 *de tironibus,* and so forth.

[39] Stein, *op. cit.,* p. 85, for the barbarian colonies *(dediticii)* and certain elements of the border garrisons; Seston, *op. cit.,* p. 330. The obligation is taken as a matter of course for the sons of all veterans in the legislation of Constantine I, e.g., *Cod. Theod.* vii. 22. 1 (313 or 319).

[40] *Cod. Theod.* vi. 24. 2 (365); vii. 1. 11 (372), 14 (394).

[41] These land grants first appear under Probus, not Septimius Severus, according to Seston, *op. cit.,* pp. 299-300. Grosse thinks that the transformation of the border garrisons into a peasantry exempt from the land tax, serving as a land-holding militia, dates from the middle of the fourth century, *op. cit.,* pp. 64-65; Seeck, "Ripariense Milites," *RE,* I², 916-18. A specially privileged class among the *limitanei* were the *castellani,* who nevertheless had a hereditary obligation to military service, Seeck, *RE,* III, 1753-54; *Cod. Theod.* vii. 15. 2 (423). The *burgarii,* however, were not soldiers but *coloni,* Seeck, "Burgus," *RE,* III, 1066-67; cf. *Cod. Theod.* xii. 19. 2 (400).

[42] Nischer, in *Heerwesen,* pp. 575-76; Grosse, *op. cit.,* pp. 203 f.; *Cod. Theod.* vii. 20. 12 (400).

[43] Liebenam, *op. cit.,* p. 631; Grosse, *op. cit.,* p. 203.

[44] It was with Theodosius I (378-95) that the barbarians definitely became the dominant element in the imperial forces, Grosse, *op. cit.,* pp. 259-65.

[45] *Cod. Theod.* vii. 22, *"de filiis militarium apparitorum et veteranorum."*

[46] *Cod. Theod.* 13. 11 (382) forbade a landholder to offer the slave of another as a recruit, implying that he might offer one of his own. See Liebenam, *op. cit.,* p. 635; Grosse, *op. cit.,* pp. 198-99. Edict ot Honorius, *Cod. Theod.* vii. 13. 16.

[47] *Ibid.,* 13. 12 (397), 17 (406). Cf. Liebenam, *op. cit.,* s. 632.

[48] *Ibid.,* 13. 3; cf. Vegetius i. 5. The Roman figures are 5' 10" and 5' 7", but the Roman foot and inch are equal to only .97 of the corresponding English measures.

[49] Grosse, *op. cit.,* p. 202; Delbrück, *op. cit.,* pp. 244-45.

[50] *Cod. Theod.* vii. 13. 6 (370), 7 § 3 (375).

[51] *Ibid.,* 1. 6 (368? 370? 373?).

[52] Cf. Amm. Marcel. xx. 8 (360), 21 (361); Zosimus ii. 15; *Cod. Theod.* vi. 27. 13 (403).

[53] Mommsen, *op. cit.,* pp. 258-59; Nischer, in *Heerwesen,* p. 581; Grosse, *op. cit.,* pp. 33-34.

[54] Delbrück, *op. cit.,* p. 294.

[55] *Ibid.,* pp. 270, 300-316; Secretan, "La Dépopulation de l'Empire romain," *Rev. hist. vaudoise,* 16 (1908), 243-44.

[56] On the civil servants in general, see "Officium," *RE,* XVII, 2 2045-46.

[57] *Cod. Theod.* xii. 1. 18 § 1 (329), vii. 22. 3 (331). According to the former of these enactments, if a son reached age thirty-five and still refused to enter his father's office, he was to be assigned to a municipal *curia* as were the sons of veterans who were physically unfit for military service (see Chap. III, above). Other laws implying the hereditary obligation are *Cod. Theod.* viii. 7. 3 (349), 15 (381), 19 (397); *Nov. Theod.* vii. 2. 2 (447). The obligation probably goes back to Diocletian.

[58] See the laws cited in note 56. Twenty years was the regular minimum length of service, cf. *RE,* XXI, 2, 2051.

[59] *RE,* XVII, 2, 2050.

[60] *Not. Dign. Occ.* xi. 38-44. For the minters, see Waltzing, *Étude historique sur les corporations professionelles chez les Romains,* II, 229-30.

[61] *Cod. Theod.* x. 20. 1, which seems to imply that their status was already well established. Also *ibid.,* 20. 10 (380), 16 (428).

[62] For Rome, Symmachus *Rel.* 29 (384/385); *Nov. Val.* iii, tit. 14, p. 1 (445). For Constantinople, *Cod. Theod.* xvi. 4. 5 § 1 (404). In general, see Waltzing, *op. cit.,* pp. 230-32; v. Premerstein, "Collectarii," *RE,* IV, 376-77, who points out that they may have operated in all large cities.

[63] On the imperial silk monopoly, see R. Lopez, "Silk Industry in the Byzantine Empire," *Speculum,* XX (1945), 1-42, particularly pp. 1-4, 10.

[64] *Not. Dign. Occ.* xi. 45-60, 62-63. See also Chap. III, above. For the operatives in these factories, see Waltzing, *op. cit.,* pp. 232-34; Hug, "Lintearius," *RE,* XIII, 717 (collection of references only).

[65] *Cod. Theod.* x. 20. 2 (357), 3 (365), 9 (380).

[66] *Ibid.,* 6 (372), also 1. 5 of the same year, 8 (374).

[67] *Ibid.,* 16 (426). Even if an individual was released from this service as a special favor upon the condition that he find a suitable substitute, he had to allow his estate to remain at the disposal of his corporation, and his family remained bound to the hereditary occupation.

[68] Dye monopoly, Gummerus, "Industrie und Handel." *RE,* IX, 1518; F. Heichelheim, *Wirtschaftsgeschichte des Altertums* (Leiden: A. W. Sijthoff, 1938), I, 821.

[69] Waltzing, *op. cit.,* pp. 234-35; Hug, "Murileguli," *RE,* XVI, 1, 662.

[70] *Cod. Theod.,* x. 20. 5.

[71] *Ibid.,* 14 (424), 15 (425).

[72] *Ibid.,* 16 (426), cited in n. 67.

[73] *Ibid.,* 6 (372), 7 (372), 8 (374), 9 (380).

[74] On the arsenals *(fabricae)* and their labor personnel *(fabricenses),* see Waltzing, *op. cit.,* pp. 239-43; Grosse, *op. cit.,* pp. 97-104; Seeck, "Fabricenses," *RE,* VI, 1925-30; *Cod. Theod.* x. 22, *de fabricensibus.*

[75] *Not. Dign. Occ.* ix. 16-39.

[76] *Cod. Theod.* x. 22. 6 (412); *Nov. Theod.* tit. 6, pr.

[77] *Ibid.*, 4 (398). Likewise the person who concealed *fabricenses* or their children was assigned to an arsenal.

[78] *Cod. Theod.* vi. 1. 8 (398).

[79] On the mines under the Late Empire, Orth, "Bergbau," *RE,* Supplb. iv, 148.

[80] *Cod. Theod.* x. 19. 1 (320), 2 (363), 8 (376), 10 (382), 11 (384); the privilege, however, came to be restricted, 13 (393).

[81] On the *metallarii,* see Waltzing, *op. cit.,* pp. 235-39; Scroff, "Marmorarius," *RE,* xiv, 1899.

[82] *Cod. Theod.* x. 19. 5 (369) ordering the arrest of those in hiding; 15 (424).

[83] *Ibid.,* ix. 40. 2 (315). These convicts were branded to make their recovery easier in case they absconded.

[84] *Ibid.,* x. 19. 3 (365).

[85] *Ibid.,* 6 (369), 7 (370? 373?), 9 (378), 15 (424).

[86] *Ibid.,* 20. 4 (368). See Waltzing, *op. cit.,* pp. 243-44; Seeck, "Bastagarii," *RE,* iii, 110.

[87] *Cod. Theod.* x. 20. 11 (384). Similar restrictions were imposed upon the employees of the state post *(cursus publicus)* and for the same reason. Cf. *Cod. Theod.* viii. 5. 58 (398); Waltzing, *op. cit.,* p. 244; Seeck, "Cursus Publicus," *RE,* iv, 1856-57.

V

[1] Possibly a shortage of recruits was one of the reasons why Septimius Severus granted soldiers permission to contract legal marriages while in service.

[2] In an agricultural economy flourishing urban communities can exist only when production greatly exceeds the needs of the producers. See Landry, *Rev. hist.,* 77, 16-18.

[3] Michigan Academy, *Annual Report,* 1939, "President's Address," pp. 39-47; *Mich. Alum. Quart. Rev.,* 1939, pp. 189-95.

[4] See Chap. i, p. ?, and n. 28.

[5] Landry, *op. cit.,* p. 23.

[6] Nischer, in *Heerwesen*, p. 478, citing L. M. Hartman and J. Kromayer, *Weltgeschichte* (Gotha, 1919), III, 170.

[7] "The Role of Policy in the Fall of the Western Empire," *Mich. Alum. Quart. Rev.*, LVI (1950), 291-94.

[8] E.g., Grosse, *Römische Militärgeschichte* . . . , pp. 200-202.

[9] *Cod. Theod.* vii. 7. 1. 2 (349?), 15 (396), 16 (396); 18. 1 (365), 2 (379), 3 (380), and the remaining fourteen laws in this section between 380 and 412.

[10] Witness the conduct of the Gauls at Mursa in 351. On decline in population and the quality of recruits, Vegetius i. 5.

[11] G. Mickwitz, *Geld und Wirtschaft* . . . (Helsingfors: Centraltryckeri och bokbinderi aktiebolag, 1932), pp. 163-64.

[12] E.g., Rostovtzeff, *Social and Economic History of the Roman Empire*, pp. 328, 484-85.

[13] Grosse, *op. cit.*, pp. 99-100.

[14] Grenier, "Gaule romaine," pp. 598-99. In my opinion Seeck's view that the importation of Germanic rural settlers reversed the downward trend in population (*Geschichte des Untergangs der römischen Welt*, I[4], 409 ff.) is untenable in the light of the evidence cited in Chaps. II-IV, above. On the relatively small number of Germans settled in southern Gaul, see R. Latouche, "Aspect demographique de la crise des grand invasions," *Population*, II (1947), 681-90.

[15] Secretan, *Rev. hist. vaudoise*, pp. 220-21, on the effects of Christian asceticism. On the question of large families, Eusebius *Demonstrat. evangel.* i. 9; cf. Piganiol, *L'Empire chrétien*, p. 412.

APPENDIX

Roman Emperors Mentioned in the Text

Early Empire or Principate

Augustus 27 B.C.–A.D. 14

Tiberius A.D. 14–37

Claudius 41–54

Vitellius 69

Trajan 98–117

Hadrian 117–138

Antoninus Pius 138–161

Marcus Aurelius 161–180

Septimius Severus 193–211

Caracalla 211–217

Severus Alexander 222–235

Gallienus 253–268

Aurelian 270–275

Probus 276–282

Later Empire or Autocracy

Diocletian A.D. 284–305

Constantine I 306–337

Constantius 337–361

Julian 360–363

Valentinian 364–375

Valens 364–378

Gratian 376–383

Theodosius I 378–395

Arcadius 383–408

Honorius 394–423

Theodosius II 408–450

Valentinian III 423–455

Marcian 455

Majorian 457–461

Severus 461–465

Anthemius 467–472

Index

Abandoned lands *(agri deserti),* 45–46, 51–52

Actors, actresses, and other entertainers, 77–78

Adjectio, *see* epibole

Africa, North, rural population of, 44–46; abandoned lands in, 45–46; urban conditions in, 61

Agathias, on army of Late Empire, 89

Alans, wanderings of, 30, 100

Alemanni, invade Italy, 24; invade the Empire, 30; settled in Po Valley, 47; ravage Gaul, 41, 60; at battle of Strassburg, 100

Ambrose, bishop, 46

Ammianus Marcellinus, 38, 58

Anthemius, 48

Aquileia, 63; mint at, 103

Aquincum, 64

Architects, lacking in Africa, 61, 77

Aristocracy, of Late Empire, 127

Arles, 58, 59, 103

Army, revolts of, 23; barbarians in, 18, 29, 115–16; of the Late Empire, 85–101, 114–16; strength of, in A.D. 235, 86–87; in A.D. 284, 87; increase under Diocletian and Constantine I, 87–91; estimated size of, in Late Empire, 88–91; recruitment of, 91–99; field troops, 94, 100;

border garrisons, 94; slaves in, 97–98; effective strength of, 100

Augustus, 5, 6, 15, 17, 65–66

Aurelian, wall of, 25; plans barbarian colonization, 28; and the dole in Rome, 66–67; and hereditary corporations, 73

Aurelius Victor, on land tax, 34

Aurileguli, 107

Ausonius, 38, 39, 58–59, 60, 63

Autun, reduction of taxes at, 40

Bagaudae, 27–28, 39, 40, 41

Barbarians, settlement of, within the Empire, 18, 27, 28, 29, 92, 96; invasions of, 24–26, 30–31, 56; settled in Britain, 38; settled in Gaul, 40, 42; in Roman army, 92, 96, 98; failure to repopulate the Empire, 127–29

Barcelona, 60

Bastagarii, 103, 107-8

Birth rate, urban, 14

Black Death, effect of, on population of England, 11; on rural population, 26

Boarii, 73

Bordeaux, 59

Braga, 60

Brigandage, in Italy, 27, 46; in Gaul, 27–28, 40–41; in Spain, 28